# Spitfire Aces of Northwest Europe 1944-45

SERIES EDITOR: TONY HOLMES

OSPREY AIRCRAFT OF THE ACES 122

# Spitfire Aces of Northwest Europe 1944-45

Andrew Thomas

**Front Cover**

From its base in the west of England, the Culmhead Wing (Nos 131 and 616 Sqns, under the leadership of Wg Cdr Peter Brothers, who had 15 victories to his name) was tasked with securing the western Channel from interference by the Luftwaffe in the days after D-Day. Both units flew the Spitfire VII, which had increased internal fuel and was fitted with extended pointed wingtips. Many of No 131 Sqn's aircraft also wore the distinctive medium grey and azure high altitude colour scheme.

Shortly after noon on 12 June Brothers led a dozen aircraft from each squadron on a 'Rodeo' (fighter sweep) from Le Mans to the south of the Normandy beachhead. Just after 1400 hrs, in a cloudless sky and in excellent visibility, the Spitfires became engaged with Bf 109s probably from I./JG 27 and Fw 190s of I./JG 11. In the ensuing combat, which saw fighters shot down by both sides, No 131 Sqn's Plt Off Bob Parry, flying as 'Black 3' in MD187/NX-V (which wore a 'high altitude' colour scheme), reported hearing an R/T call of 'Huns about' and then spotted a Bf 109 heading south at very low level about a mile west of the airfield at Laval. With his No 2, Flt Sgt Kelley, he gave chase. The unit's combat report recounted the subsequent action;

'Parry half-rolled down on it from the starboard side. The pilot evidently saw him, for he dropped his jettison tank and turned slowly towards Parry, who had no difficulty in getting in astern at the same height and giving him a one-second burst from 200 yards. Strikes were seen all over the cockpit and on both wing roots. The starboard wing folded back and the enemy aircraft began to roll over onto its back. The port wing broke off and the remainder of the enemy aircraft crashed in the back garden of a house about one mile southwest of the airfield. Flt Sgt Kelley ("Black 4") followed Flg Off Parry down and confirms this.'

In claiming his first victory Bob Parry had fired 120 rounds from his cannon and 500 from his machine guns.

Despite the losses it had been a successful day for the Culmhead Wing. However, low-level operations put an increased strain on the extended wingtips, so five days later

First published in Great Britain in 2014 by Osprey Publishing
PO Box 883, Oxford, OX1 9PL, UK
PO Box 3985, New York, NY 10185-3985, USA

E-mail: info@ospreypublishing.com

Osprey Publishing is part of the Osprey Group

© 2014 Osprey Publishing Limited

A CIP catalogue record for this book is available from the British Library

ISBN: 978 1 78200 338 0
PDF e-book ISBN: 978 1 78200 339 7
e-Pub ISBN: 978 1 78200 340 3

Edited by Tony Holmes
Cover Artwork by Mark Postlethwaite
Aircraft Profiles by Chris Thomas
Index by Zoe Ross
Originated by PDQ Digital Media Solutions, UK
Printed in China through Asia Pacific Offset Limited

14 15 16 17 18   10 9 8 7 6 5 4 3 2 1

Osprey Publishing is supporting the Woodland Trust, the UK's leading woodland conservation charity, by funding the dedication of trees.

www.ospreypublishing.com

Parry and Flt Lt Cliff Rudland flew a comparative trial with two aircraft, one with the pointed 'high altitude' tips and the other with the more usual 'rounded' tips. The trial showed that the latter were better suited for the lower level environment, and over the next few days all the aircraft were changed and the pointed tips saw little use thereafter. This specially commissioned cover painting by Mark Postlethwaite shows Parry's fire from his extended wingtip Spitfire setting the Messerschmitt on fire before it disintegrated and crashed

# CONTENTS

# EARLY ENCOUNTERS

'At about 1325 hrs at 22,000 ft I saw two '190s attacking a straggling Fort. I dived to attack and one of the '190s, after delivering his attack, climbed away into the sun and towards myself and my section. He obviously did not see us and started to turn in for another attack. I opened fire from 400 yards with machine guns and cannon. The enemy aircraft started to half-roll and dive down. I followed, closing to 150-200 yards, and saw strikes followed by a burst of flames from beneath his cockpit. I lost sight under my nose as I had been firing on my back. I broke upwards. When I looked down again I saw an open parachute.'

Thus did the former Cranwell Cadet and leader of No 125 Airfield, New Zealander Wg Cdr Bob Yule, describe his eighth, and final, victory that was also to be the first of many by an ace whilst flying a Merlin-engined Spitfire during 1944. His success came while leading elements of Nos 132 and 602 Sqns from Detling, in Kent, during the early afternoon of 7 January 1944. The Spitfire pilots were providing withdrawal cover to USAAF heavy bombers, and they had been vectored to support the third 'box' that was reportedly in trouble. Also successful was Flt Lt Harry Walmsley of No 132 Sqn, who, flying Spitfire IX MH719/FF-J, claimed the second of his 12 victories;

'After the initial fight about ten miles east of Abbeville, four FW 190s started to chase me. I called for assistance and then saw four more in front of me, heading for the coast. Having a considerable advantage in speed, I attacked the rear one at 250 yards from line astern. He started to turn to port and I hit him in the port cowling and cockpit. He went down immediately on fire. The remaining three then attacked me, and at this stage Wg Cdr Yule arrived with his section, for which I was extremely grateful!'

Two Fw 190s from *Jagdgeschwader* 26 were indeed shot down, as the unit lost four aircraft that afternoon, the others falling to P-47s of the USAAF's 4th Fighter Group (FG).

No 125 Airfield was part of the 2nd Tactical Air Force (TAF), which had been formed on 15 November 1943 from an amalgam of the tactical elements of Fighter Command, the tactical bombers of Bomber Command's No 2 Group and the squadrons of Army Co-operation Command. Its task was to give direct support to land forces following the coming invasion of France, and to move with them during the subsequent advance into Northwest Europe. The remainder of Fighter Command was re-titled the Air Defence of Great Britain (ADGB), and it retained responsibility for homeland air defence.

2nd TAF Airfields (later re-titled as Wings) were equipped to be highly mobile, and had been training and conducting operations through the summer of 1943. 2nd TAF's tactical fighter squadrons were controlled by two group HQs (Nos 83 and 84 Groups), each of which would give direct support to the two armies that were to comprise the Anglo-Canadian 21st Army Group following the invasion of France.

The first ace to claim a victory in a Spitfire in 1944 was the No 125 Airfield Leader Wg Cdr Bob Yule, who on the afternoon of 7 January claimed his final success when he shot down an Fw 190 near Abbeville (*via Norman Franks*)

When 2nd TAF formed, 23 of its 32 single-engined fighter or fighter-bomber squadrons flew the Spitfire, and by May 1945 44 squadrons of Merlin-engined Spitfires had been under its command at some stage. A further 20 squadrons had flown exclusively with ADGB (which after D-Day reverted to the name Fighter Command), undertaking UK-based air defence and bomber escort duties. These numbers clearly illustrate the pre-eminence of the Spitfire in the RAF, Commonwealth and 'Free European' air forces.

At this stage 2nd TAF units were commanded by highly experienced pilots, most of whom were aces, and this level of expertise would continue. For example, No 125 Airfield was under the overall command of Gp Capt Jamie Rankin, who had 23 victories to his name, and was led in the air by Wg Cdr Bob Yule, whilst the Polish No 131 Airfield was commanded by 11-victory ace Gp Capt Alexander Gabszewicz and led by Wg Cdr Stanislaw Skalski, who eventually claimed 21 kills.

Flt Lt Warren Peglar of No 501 Sqn, who later became an Eighth Air Force ace, summarised the activities of the Spitfire units at this time to the author specifically for this volume;

'As we entered into 1944 the tempo of our war in the air increased. We were now escorting medium bombers into France and Belgium, bombing railway junctions, airfields, harbours, etc. And, during this time, the pace of the RAF night bombing and the USAAF day bombing increased mightily. Night and day the drone of heavy aircraft overhead continued. We pressed ever deeper into France, Belgium and Holland and we attacked trains, shipping, anti-aircraft positions and – something new – buzz-bomb installations! These were being built up in quantity, and eventually they were used to fire unmanned missiles at England in great number from June 1944.'

Action in 1944 began for the Spitfire units on the afternoon of 2 January when Flt Sgt A E van den Broeck of No 349 Sqn, flying Spitfire VB BL565/GE-E, was lost to an Fw 190 of 4./JG 26 flown by Feldwebel Gerd Weigand over the Channel during a 'Rhubarb' near the Somme estuary. A 'Rhubarb' was the RAF Fighter Command term used to describe an operation when sections of fighters or fighter-bombers, taking full advantage of low cloud and poor visibility, would cross the English Channel and then drop below cloud level to search for opportunity targets such as railway locomotives and rolling stock, aircraft on the ground, enemy troops and vehicles on roads.

There were further skirmishes on the 4th, with the first confirmed Spitfire victory of the year coming two days later. It fell to No 19 Sqn flying from Gravesend (this unit would soon relinquish its Spitfire IXs for Mustang IIIs) when escorting bombers hitting V1 targets in the Poix area. Near Rouen shortly after midday, Flt Sgt D A Hutchinson (in MH365) shot down an 'Fw 190' and damaged

One of the most impressive scoreboards on a Spitfire was worn on MH883/VZ-B of No 412 Sqn, denoting the 32 victories of Flt Lt George Beurling. The most successful Allied fighter pilot over Malta briefly served with No 412 Sqn at Biggin Hill from late November 1943 until February 1944, claiming his final victory – in this aircraft – with the unit on 30 December (*via C H Thomas*)

two more, whilst future Mustang ace Flt Sgt Basilios Vassiliades had the frustration of lining up on one and on pressing the gun button getting no response whatsoever!

The Royal Canadian Air Force (RCAF) squadrons that would subsequently achieve so much success in 2nd TAF were not far behind No 19 Sqn, for 20 minutes later, at 1230 hrs, a joint sweep by Nos 401 and 411 Sqns from Biggin Hill encountered more 'Fw 190s' east of Rouen. Over Pavilly Flt Lt Russ Orr of the latter unit broke to starboard and chased them from 18,000 ft down to deck level, where one of the enemy fighters tried to outturn the Spitfire. He fired three bursts, the last of which hit the cockpit, causing the fighter to flick roll several times before crashing into a wood for the first of Orr's three victories. The opponents in both of these actions were not Fw 190s, however, for Bf 109G-equipped II. and III./JG 2 lost three aircraft on this date.

Attacks on what were later known to be V1 launching sites were a priority, and flak around them took a steady toll such as on 9 January when Flg Off 'Tex' Davenport of No 401 was shot down near Hesdin. He evaded and later returned to become an ace.

The Luftwaffe often hotly opposed these 'Ramrods' (short-range bomber attacks to destroy ground targets, similar to 'Circus' missions that saw bombers attacking with fighter escorts), such as on the 14th when RAF fighters escorted USAAF B-26 Marauders. Near Hesdin, Spitfires from Nos 19, 122, 132 and 602 Sqns, led by Wg Cdr Yule, spotted some Bf 109s. Yule led No 132 Sqn down to attack, claiming a Bf 109 damaged, while Flt Lt Smith shot down an Fw 190. A few moments later No 602 Sqn also became embroiled and, flying Spitfire IX MJ147, Flt Lt Ken Charney shot down an Fw 190 to record his fourth victory. Sadly, when the formation egressed at low-level over the French coast near Berck-sur-Mer, No 132 Sqn's CO, Sqn Ldr Franz Colloredo-Mansfeld, who was of Austrian and US extraction and had a total of 11 claims to his name, was hit by flak and crashed to his death. He was replaced a few days later by Sqn Ldr Geoffrey Page, an ace who would more than double his score during his tenure. Both Nos 132 and 602 Sqns were posted to northern Scotland for defence duties just as Page assumed command.

Some of the first Spitfire victories of 1944 were claimed by No 602 Sqn, whose pilots came together for this group shot at Detling in mid January. Frenchman, and future ace, Asp Pierre Clostermann is sat in the cockpit of MH909/LO-R (*via Dugald Cameron*)

Dane Lt Col Kaj Birksted, who claimed the last of his 11 victories on 23 January 1944, led the Norwegian Wing. He later commanded a Mustang Wing (*R C Hay*)

Spitfire IX MA568/FN-L belonged to No 331 (Norwegian) Sqn, and on 29 January 1944 it was flown on a 'Ramrod' bomber escort mission by future ace 2Lt Ragnar Dogger (*S Heglund via Cato Guhnfeld*)

Sweeps continued almost daily, and at 1240 hrs on 21 January Malta ace Plt Off Claude Weaver of No 403 Sqn shot down an Fw 190 near Lens to claim his 13th success. Thirty minutes later Wg Cdr Reg Grant, in his personal Spitfire IX MH851/RJG, led Nos 19 and 122 Sqns of No 122 Airfield on a sweep. At 18,000 ft near St Pol he spotted a 'Me 210' and gave chase, scoring many hits, to be followed by others before it went down. His share in the aircraft gave Grant his eighth, and final, victory. No 122 Airfield then stood down to re-equip with the Mustang III, but other Spitfires continued to see action.

On 23 January the Norwegians of No 132 Airfield, led by Lt Col Kaj Birksted, along with the Poles from No 134 Airfield escorted Marauders on a 'Ramrod'. As the formation approached Amiens at 1545 hrs the Norwegians spotted four Fw 190s. They chased the enemy fighters as far as Breteuil, shooting down three of them. One fell to Birksted as his 11th, and last, victory;

'We engaged four FW 190s flying north at 22,000 ft directly below us. I dived down, picking one FW 190 that broke 180 degrees to starboard. Turning inside him, I fired a short burst while closing from 400 yards, overshooting him slightly. He did a complete barrel roll, and a cylindrical tank that was on fire and pouring out petrol came off. Rolling with him, I followed him in a steep dive to 12,000 ft, where he levelled off and climbed very steeply back to 22,000 ft. Here, he levelled off in a slight starboard turn as if to bail out. Closing rapidly again, I fired the rest of my cannon from 300 down to 100 yards. I saw one big flash on his underside, flames shooting out. He fell slowly over into a vertical dive. I followed him down to 10,000 ft, using the remainder of my machine gun ammunition. He was emitting slight fire and thin white smoke from under his engine. I broke away at 10,000 ft, my No 2, Gp Capt Robinson, continuing to fire at him. I watched them still going down to 5000 ft, when Gp Capt Robinson broke away.'

Lt Ragnar Dogger of No 331 Sqn, flying Spitfire IX MH940/FN-D, was also successful, claiming the second of his six victories. The third Focke-Wulf fell to the combined fire of Sgt Riung and Maj Werner Christie, who attacked one Fw 190 and then went after another. He gave the following account of what happened next in his combat report;

'As I broke away from this first attack my No 2 and I broke round to starboard. I saw a FW 190 followed by two Spitfires, and as I was in a very convenient position I cut in front of the Spitfires. I had a short burst out of range but then caught up and opened fire from 500 yards, and so did my No 2, who was in line abreast with me. I saw several good cannon strikes on both wing roots. The enemy aircraft was smoking heavily and appeared to be out of control when I broke off the attack at 15,000 ft. This same enemy aircraft was seen afterwards diving down in flames.'

This shared victory made the 26-year-old the first Spitfire pilot to achieve acedom in 1944.

On the debit side, however, during a sweep on 28 January the 20-year-old American ace Claude Weaver was shot down by fellow ace Oberleutnant Gerhard Vogt of 7./JG 26. Although he managed to bail out his parachute became entangled on the tail of his aircraft and Weaver was dragged to his death. He was the first Spitfire ace to be killed in 1944.

## HIGH FLIERS

The ADGB squadrons were also active, and though most, like their 2nd TAF brethren, flew Spitfire IXs, some still remained equipped with the earlier Mk VB. Many of the latter were of the clipped wing variety, leading to them being unflatteringly described as 'cropped, clipped and clapped'! Amongst those flying the aircraft was No 234 Sqn, whose OC 'B' Flight was 24-year-old Flt Lt 'Wally' Walton. Over Malta in 1942 he had made 15 claims, including six destroyed. Although tee total, Walton had a reputation of leading from the front – both in the air and at a party!

From Coltishall No 234 Sqn flew 'Jim Crows' (coastal patrols to intercept enemy aircraft crossing the British coastline) over the North Sea and escorted Beaufighter anti-shipping strikes. Other ADGB units, including Nos 124, 131 and 616 Sqns, flew the Spitfire VII that was pressurised and optimised for high altitude operations. Up at their lonely outpost at Skeabrae, in Orkney, for protection of the Royal Navy anchorage at Scapa Flow, No 602 Sqn also had a trio of Mk VIIs alongside its Mk Vs. On 20 February 26-year-old Plt Off Ian Blair was scrambled in Spitfire VII MD114/DU-G, as he described in an interview many years later;

'We scrambled to intercept a high-flying Me 109 on a recce. In my logbook I have written, "Scramble – 26 min to Tally Ho! Aircraft destroyed". I was in a Spitfire VII, which had a pressure cabin, and we climbed smartly up to 32,000 ft and spotted a vapour trail at "12 o'clock". We got to 38,000 ft, as this aircraft was phenomenal – it had pointy wingtips. The Hun turned and dived to starboard at an indicated airspeed of 500 mph. I had two squirts at 1000 yards then my No 2 passed and closed to 300 yards in the stern, but missed – in fact his guns failed to fire. I then had a go – just three seconds at 100

The first pilot to become an ace in the Spitfire in 1944 was the CO of No 332 Sqn, 26-year-old Norwegian Maj Werner Christie, seen here during January of that year (*P H T Green collection*)

Among the units still flying the 'clipped wing' Spitfire VB at the start of 1944 was Coltishall-based No 234 Sqn, whose B Flight was led by six-victory ace Flt Lt Wally Walton (*P H T Green collection*)

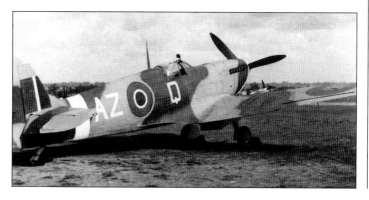

After moving to Skeabrae from Detling in mid-January 1944, No 602 Sqn flew three Spitfire VIIs alongside its Mk VBs on high-altitude interceptions. MD114/DU-G was used by Plt Off Ian Blair to shoot down a reconnaissance Bf 109 at 38,000 ft on 20 February (*The Orkney Library, Kirkwall*)

This camera gun image shows Ian Blair's shells sending Oberleutnant Helmut Quednau's Bf 109 to destruction off the Orkneys (*Ian Blair via Dugald Cameron*)

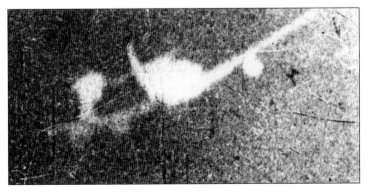

yards. The starboard wing blew off and the aircraft crashed in the drink with no sign of the pilot. I was struck by pieces of wreckage and coolant started to leak out.

'I was half way to Norway – it was a nice day and you could see the Norwegian coastline. I cooled the engine down and managed to get back to Stronsay Island – a little bit north of Skeabrae. I literally landed in a field about 1200 yards long, 20 ft above sea level. I put it down in a peat bog, and the two radiators dug a furrow that resulted in me getting two black eyes and a cut on the bridge of my nose after I struck the gunsight. We got a good report from the Navy and the Admiral wanted to see me and congratulate me. Worked out quite good!'

Blair's victim was Bf 109G-6/R-3 Wk-Nr 20357/A6+XH of 1(F)./120, flown by Oberleutnant Helmut Quednau, who had taken off from Stavanger on a reconnaissance mission to Scapa Flow.

2nd TAF squadrons also continued to be active into February, with the Norwegians in action again on the 11th when ace Lt Frederik Fearnley of No 331 Sqn increased his score whilst covering a USAAF B-17 raid;

'I closed in as we dived from 26,000 ft to 6000 ft and gave the nearest FW 190 numerous short bursts from 400 yards. I saw strikes on the starboard wing and on the underside of the fuselage. Small explosions with flames and black smoke came from the aircraft, and then its starboard wing broke off. It fell away in an uncontrollable vertical spin into cloud, leaving a puff of black smoke on the top of the cloud at about 4000 ft.'

Sadly, Fearnley was killed by flak while strafing St Trond airfield on 25 February.

Eleven days earlier, No 401 Sqn's CO, Sqn Ldr Lorne Cameron, had led a 'Ranger' to France. During the course of this mission Newfoundlander Flg Off Bob Hayward began his path to acedom;

'I spotted an aircraft at about 4000 ft. He must have spotted me as he dived about 30 degrees to the deck. While closing at high revs and boost, my engine cut out and my overtaking speed dropped considerably. I opened up at a range of 400 to 500 yards from dead astern. My engine cut out again, so I held for a long burst, during which I saw strikes on the fuselage, port engine and wing root to the starboard side. The port engine became enveloped in flames and I pulled up above him.'

The 'Me 210' (almost certainly a Me 410) crashed east of St André airfield.

# PREPARING FOR INVASION

As spring approached, and with the advent of improving weather, the Allied air forces increased the tempo of operations in preparation for the coming invasion, spurred on by the knowledge that it was now about when, not if, it would begin. For the tactical air forces, their primary mission was to knock out coastal defences, including gun batteries and radar sites, and target rail and road links into the coastal areas so as to prevent the enemy from rapidly concentrating forces against the landings. The might of Bomber Command was also made available to strike at pre-invasion targets, and when they operated by day, the bombers would do so under heavy fighter escort.

Additionally, the evolving threat posed by the as yet unused V1 flying bomb sites in the Pas de Calais area had to be neutralised as a priority. Often sited in woods, and well camouflaged, these were proving to be difficult and dangerous targets, for not only were they hard to detect, they were ringed with anti-aircraft defences that were exacting a heavy toll on the attacking fighters.

Through the winter and spring of 1944 all 2nd TAF Spitfire units continued training for the ground attack role, being detached to an Armament Practice Camp at Llanbedr or Fairwood Common, in Wales, or Hutton Cranswick, in Yorkshire, for one to two weeks to receive instruction and to hone their skills in air-to-air and air-to-ground gunnery and in the art of dive-bombing. Few fighter pilots had any experience of dive-bombing, and it was not universally welcomed. However, the intense training conducted prior to and after the invasion was to pay dividends in the maelstrom of fighting they were to encounter. Seldom was the phrase of 'train hard, fight easy' more appropriate.

2nd TAF's Spitfire squadrons were a cosmopolitan collection, with Free French, Norwegian, Polish and Czech wings (as the Airfields were later re-titled) eventually coming under its command, whilst individual Belgian and Dutch squadrons served in RAF wings, as did Royal Australian Air Force (RAAF) and Royal New Zealand Air Force (RNZAF) Spitfire squadrons. However, after the RAF, by far the largest contributor was the RCAF, which in early 1944 had sent six more fighter squadrons to Britain, some with operational experience against the Japanese in the Aleutians, from the Home Establishment and three of these received Spitfires. Indeed, such was their pre-eminence during the campaign in Northwest Europe that of the 38 pilots that claimed five or more victories flying Merlin-engined Spitfires during 1944-45, all but four were from the RCAF!

It was the Poles that drew first blood in March, however, as over Creil airfield during the late afternoon of the 1st Sgt Rybczynski of No 308 Sqn shot down an Fw 190. That day was also important for the Frenchmen of

**At the start of 1944 Flt Lt Jack Sheppard, who had previously flown catapult Hurricanes from merchant ships, was serving with No 401 Sqn. In April he became CO of No 412 Sqn, with whom he became an ace in July (*DND*)**

No 341 (Alsace) Sqn, as Cne Christian Martel (a *nomme de guerre* for Pierre Montet), the flight commander who had gained seven victories during 1943 and who became the unit CO on 3 April, recalled;

'On 1 March we gave up our Spitfire Vs and received the Spitfire IX. I flew my first operation on the 6th – a scramble from readiness, but without success. Two weeks after receiving our Mk IXs the order came to move to Merston, opposite the Isle of Wight. Our Wing was to join 2nd TAF.'

The Canadians opened their account on the 7th near Beaumont-sur-Oise, as the No 401 Sqn diarist recorded;

'Over France Flt Lt Sheppard saw an FW 190 on the deck just over the perimeter track and went down on it, with his section following. He engaged the Hun at treetop level and shot it down. As the squadron was climbing back up, Flg Off Klersy spotted another FW 190 on the deck and went down. He had several good bursts from 200 to 100 yards and the Hun finally half-rolled into the ground in flames.'

The latter aircraft was the first of 22-year-old Bill Klersy's 15 victories, whilst Jack Sheppard's Fw 190 was the second of his five victories. These attacks were no sinecure, however, as the heavy and accurate flak encountered by No 403 Sqn when strafing motor transport near St Aurore de l'Eure the following day cost it two aircraft, including the Spitfire IX flown by Malta ace Flg Off Jim Ballantyne, who was killed.

Their compatriots in the Spitfire squadrons under ADGB command flew defensive patrols, bomber escorts and fighter sweeps to continue the attrition of the Luftwaffe in France and Belgium. Their major priority though was 'blinding the enemy' by preventing reconnaissance of southern England in order to prevent the Germans from gauging the extent of the Allied pre-invasion build up. The high-flying Spitfire VII units had an important part to play in this task, with pilots like Flg Off Bert Yeardley of No 124 Sqn at West Malling being in the vanguard of operations. On the morning of 25 February he and his wingman were on patrol when an intruder was spotted;

'The section was off Dungeness at 24,000 ft on vector 100 when Sgt Clarke sighted vapour trails above at about 30-40 miles ahead, travelling southwest. The section dropped auxiliary tanks, opened up full boost and revs and crossed the French coast at Sangatte at 27,000 ft. We crossed beneath the aircraft and came in behind it, quickly recognising the contact as hostile through its black crosses, although we could not identify what type of aeroplane it was. By diving and pulling up we managed to close the range, and as a result of the attack the enemy aircraft was seen to crash in a wood about 15 miles south of Calais.'

Yeardley was credited with downing a Ju 88 for the second of his three victories.

No 616 Sqn was also equipped with the high-altitude Spitfire VII, the unit having replaced No 124 Sqn at West Malling in mid-March. One of its flight commanders was 11-victory ace Flt Lt Garry Nowell, who had been badly wounded in 1940 and who flew his first operation with No 616 in YQ-K on the 18th when he undertook a defensive patrol off Dungeness. On the evening of the 25th, in YQ-E, he was scrambled as Blue section leader, but found nothing significant to report.

Attacks on enemy targets continued, with 2nd TAF units regularly encountering German aircraft during the course of these missions. One such occasion was on 15 March, when the Canadian-manned Nos 126 and 127 Airfields covered an attack by 72 B-26s on the marshalling yards at Aulnoy. As the formation neared Cambrai six Fw 190s were spotted attempting to land. In the ensuing 'bounce' by No 401 Sqn four were shot down, with both Flt Lt Jack Sheppard and Flg Off Bob Hayward continuing on their paths to acedom. A week later, on the 23rd, during a 'Ramrod' by No 126 Airfield escorting 72 B-26s to rail marshalling yards at Creil, Flg Off Don Laubman of No 412 Sqn, flying Spitfire IX MJ230, spotted a Ju 88 below him. In company with Flt Lt W B Needham, he dived after the aircraft and both pilots shot it down. This was the first victory for the 22-year-old Laubman, who would subsequently become the most successful Spitfire pilot of the post-D-Day campaign in Northwest Europe. His aircraft was, however, hit by return fire and had to crash land at Kenley while attempting to reach Biggin Hill.

It was not all work though, as the No 421 Sqn diarist noted on 25 March;

'Flg Off Andy Mackenzie's big day dawned bright and clear. The fatal words were pronounced at 1332 hrs. A party commenced, followed by many drinks and much kissing of the bride. As time wore on the party became somewhat rougher, with the groom thrown in the swimming pool followed by several of the pushers. Here's to many years of health, wealth and happiness to Mac and Joyce.'

The toast came to fruition as 'Mac' Mackenzie later took his total to eight destroyed and, post-war, became the president of the Canadian Fighter Pilots' Association.

The three recently arrived RCAF units, Nos 441, 442 and 443 Sqns, each of which had an experienced CO, became the newly formed No 144 Airfield at Hutton Cranswick. The Wing Leader was none other than the formidable Wg Cdr 'Johnnie' Johnson, who already had 21 and seven shared victories to his name. He led the new wing on its first operation on 28 March, which saw Dreux airfield strafed in a combat debut for a

Heavily weathered Spitfire IX MH852/NX-Z belonged to Culmhead-based No 131 Sqn. It was regularly flown during March 1944 by Flt Lt Cliff Rudland, who had enjoyed success flying Whirlwind Is with No 263 Sqn in 1941. No 131 Sqn replaced its Spitfire IXs with high-altitude Spitfire VIIs shortly after this photograph was taken (*Keith Saunders*)

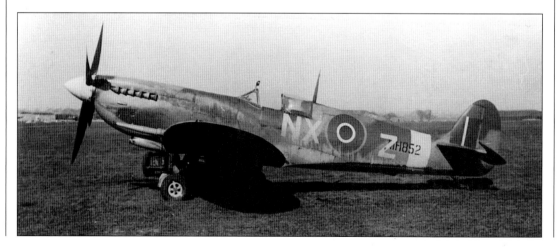

number of pilots who would become aces in the succeeding months. Their countrymen in No 127 Airfield started a new role in early April as was reported in the Canadian press at the time;

'Canada's Wolf Squadron used its Spitfires in a new role – as fighter-bombers – on Saturday, when bombs were dropped on a military target in northern France. Airmen said the only opposition was negligible flak, and all but one bomb landed in the target area. "It was all over in three minutes", said one pilot from St Catherine's. "Then we circled a couple of times and came home in formations, leaving a column of black smoke rising 1000 ft. We peeled down one after the other in a 5000-ft dive, and each let his bombs go as he reached the bottom. I could see mine land one after the other as they exploded right in the target area.'

RAF units too were in the thick of it, typical being No 132 Sqn led by Sqn Ldr Geoffrey Page that gave close escort to B-26s attacking E-boat pens at Ijmuiden and rail targets in Belgium and northern France through late March and into April, for which he used his regular Spitfire IX MK144/FF-O.

Although the bulk of the Spitfire squadrons were based at airfields and, increasingly, on Advanced Landing Grounds (ALG) in the southeast, others were situated further west. In April No 10 Group ADGB was reorganised, as 15-victory ace Wg Cdr Peter Brothers explained;

'In April 1944 I was given command of a Wing that consisted of Nos 610 (Spitfire XIV), 616 (Spitfire VII) and 131 (Spitfire VII) Sqns at Culmhead, No 41 Sqn (Spitfire XII) at Bolt Head, No 126 Sqn (Spitfire IXB) at Exeter and No 263 Sqn (Typhoon) at Harrowbeer. They were too scattered to control, so I moved No 126 Sqn to Culmhead and subsequently persuaded Tommy Dalton-Morgan [Operations Officer, HQ No 10 Group] to rename us the Culmhead Wing, and form a Harrowbeer Wing using No 126 Sqn, whose fighters had less range than our Spitfire XIVs and VIIs. "Birdy" [Wg Cdr H A C Bird-Wilson, an ace with eight victories] came and took over the new wing. Either wing might be required for escort duties, either for our own medium daylight bombers, fighter-bombers or the American "heavies".'

## INCREASING TEMPO

Throughout April the operational tempo quickened, and despite some wing leaders quickly becoming tour expired, the quality of leadership was maintained. For example, in No 126 Airfield Wg Cdr 'Buck' McNair left, having been awarded the DSO, and Wg Cdr George Keefer was brought in as his replacement – between them, the two pilots would claim 28 victories. Keefer's place as OC No 412 Sqn was taken by newly promoted Sqn Ldr Jack Sheppard, whose friend and fellow future ace Bob Hayward described as being a 'cool and calculating fighter pilot who did not agree with strafing the enemy on the ground'.

Another command change took place in No 442 Sqn, where Sqn Ldr Brad Walker was replaced by Battle of Britain ace Sqn Ldr Dal Russel.

Wg Cdr Johnson's No 144 Airfield also broke its duck at this time. When leading a sweep by No 443 Sqn on the evening of 19 April Johnson spotted a Do 217. He also noted that No 443 Sqn's aggressive CO, Sqn Ldr Wally McLeod, was flying alongside him, as Johnson described in his autobiography;

In early 1944 the RCAF transferred several fighter squadrons to 2nd TAF from Canada. One became No 442 Sqn, which in May 1944 came under the command of Battle of Britain ace Sqn Ldr Dal Russel. Having claimed his final victory soon after D-Day, Russel then led No 126 Wing until early 1945 (*DND*)

'I said "It's yours Wally. Let's see how you do it!" He closed for the kill and the rest of us hung back to watch the duel. It was all over in a flash. There was no tearing pursuit. No twisting and weaving as the bomber tried to escape. It was a classic example of fine shooting with a master of the craft in the Spitfire. Wally nailed his victim with the first burst and the Dornier pulled up steeply so that we saw it

No 165 Sqn formed part of the ADGB with the Spitfire IX, including MH826/SK-N that it flew on sweeps and escorts over northern France before the invasion. This fighter later served with No 453 Sqn (*author's collection*)

in plan view, hung for a moment in the air and then fell on its side and crashed with a sheet of flame near the back gardens of a row of cottages.'

It was McLeod's 14th victory, and he subsequently became the most successful RCAF pilot of World War 2.

ADGB gained a new Spitfire unit in early April when No 1 Sqn at North Weald began replacing its Typhoons with Mk IXs and gained a new CO in New Zealand ace Sqn Ldr Johnny Checketts. Later in the month it moved down to Predannack, where it formed a wing with No 165 Sqn for 'Instep' patrols (missions to restrict attacks on RAF Coastal Command aircraft by maintaining a presence over the Western Approaches and flying operations over western France). Also, following Checketts' promotion, another ace, South African Sqn Ldr Pat Lardner-Burke, assumed command. At the other end of the country Flt Sgt Jim Thorne of No 504 Sqn, in Spitfire V BL907, shared in the destruction of a Ju 88 northeast of the Orkneys in a rare engagement in that area. He later became an ace flying Mustang IIIs.

Most action during this period took place over France of course, and on a clear morning on 25 April Johnson, in MK392/JE-J, led Nos 441 and 443 Sqns on a 'Ramrod' to the Paris area ahead of an attack by USAAF B-24s. Enemy fighters were spotted near Laon, and Johnson went straight in with Plt Off Luis Perez-Gomez covering his tail;

'I identified the aircraft as Fw 190s flying in line abreast. I ordered Blue Section to attack the port enemy aircraft and led Red Section to attack the starboard. I attacked the leader. As I attacked he half-rolled and I half-rolled too, continuing my fire from 300 yards.'

Perez-Gomez wrote, 'I saw black smoke and it didn't recover from its dive. Finally, the fighter crashed in the middle of a bush and blew up'. His leader was not yet finished, however;

'I followed another Fw 190 down to ground level. After 15-20 miles at ground level he eased up. I closed to 250 yards and gave him several short bursts. Strikes were seen and the enemy aircraft turned to port, climbed steeply to 700 ft and then fell to the ground in a straight dive.'

Other pilots claimed four more victims, including the 17th victory for No 441 Sqn's CO Sqn Ldr George Hill. Flying Spitfire IX MK519, he shared one with Flg Off Sparling, although the latter pilot was forced to ditch on the way back, whilst Hill, whose fighter had been shot up by another Fw 190, crash-landed near Laon. He evaded capture and made it as far as the Spanish border, where he was arrested and handed over to the Gestapo. Hill endured extreme brutality at their hands for a full six

At the turn of the year Free French ace Lt Robert Gouby was serving with No 165 Sqn, although he subsequently moved to No 611 Sqn and claimed his final victory with the latter unit shortly after D-Day. He was one of many aces that later fell victim to enemy flak (*via C-J Ehrengard*)

months before being transferred to a Luftwaffe-run PoW camp. He was succeeded by Sqn Ldr Danny Browne. No 144 Airfield's aerial combat debut had thus been a day of mixed fortunes, and another ace fell 24 hours later when, returning from a sweep with his Free French Wing, Wg Cdr Roy Marples collided with a wingman and was killed.

In the run-up to the invasion several experienced fighter squadrons arrived in England from the Mediterranean and were re-equipped with Spitfires. In No 11 Group No 80 Sqn, under the command of Norwegian ace Maj Bjorn Bjornstad, with 19 new Spitfire IXs, moved to Detling and formed a wing with Nos 229 and 274 Sqns, the latter led by Canadian ace Sqn Ldr Eddie Edwards. The overall Wing Leader was New Zealand ace Wg Cdr Edward 'Hawkeye' Wells. No 80 Sqn commenced operations on 7 May when seven aircraft joined a 'Ramrod' escorting bombers to Berck, and this set the scene for activities in the run up to the invasion.

Another unit brought back to England was No 74 Sqn, led by five-victory New Zealand ace Sqn Ldr Jim 'Spud' Hayter. It formed a wing at Lympne with Nos 33 and 127 Sqns, the latter flying its first fighter-bomber sorties over France on 19 May.

Meanwhile, 'Johnnie' Johnson's No 144 Airfield had gained more success when he led a sweep in support of a raid on Lille on 5 May. At 0745 hrs he spotted enemy aircraft, and his combat report described the action as follows;

'When over Douai I saw six FW 190s flying over the town at ground level. I detached No 443 Sqn to go down and search for them. About five minutes afterwards I saw a FW 190 flying west at 2000 ft. I closed from its port side and opened fire from 300 yards, closing to five degrees angle off. After a one-second burst the enemy aircraft jettisoned its hood and tank and pieces were seen to fly off. I continued to fire and the pilot bailed out at 400 ft, and, unfortunately, landed safely by parachute.'

The Spitfire formation then flew on to Mons where, at 0820 hrs, more Fw 190s were attacked. Two were shot down, one of which fell to North Africa ace Flt Lt Freddie Wilson of No 441 Sqn in Mk IX MK399/9G-K. This was his ninth, and last, victory. No 443 Sqn's Wally McLeod noted, 'It rolled onto its back and went straight in, exploding when it hit the ground'. Plt Off Gamey got the other Fw 190 – both Feldwebel Horst Schwentick and Unteroffizier Manfred Talkenberg of 5./JG 26 were killed. A few minutes later McLeod, who was flying Spitfire IX MK636/2I-E, despatched another near Brussels;

'We bounced from line astern but the enemy aircraft saw us and broke sharply to port. A general mêlée ensued. I observed one FW 190 being shot down by a Spitfire in a turn. I selected a FW 190 that left the gaggle and chased him due east for ten minutes at treetop height. He finally pulled up to 1000 ft and broke to port. I cut the corner, firing a two-second burst from 150 yards. Strikes were observed on the cowling and cockpit. Smoke and fire was observed and the enemy aircraft rolled onto its back and started in. I fired another short burst (1.5 seconds) from line astern at 175 yards – the enemy aircraft burst completely into flames and crashed, exploding.'

Two days later the activities of units from Nos 126 and 127 Airfields (Nos 411 and 403 Sqns, respectively) once again received coverage in the Canadian press;

'Canadian Spitfires patrolling over France today blew three enemy fighters from the sky, with Flt Lt Russell Orr of 206 Livingstone Ave, Toronto, getting two within five seconds. The other fell to Flt Lt J D Lindsay of Arnprior, Ontario, marking his first kill. Lindsay, flying with the Wolf squadron, got an ME 109 in approximately the same area as four enemy aeroplanes pounced on the Canadians. Lindsay went after one pair, selecting his target because "he looked dumbest of the two", and gave him a five-second burst. A wing snapped off the enemy craft and its hood blew up.'

Seen at dispersal before D-Day, Spitfire IX ML411/KH-Z of No 403 Sqn was used to good effect throughout the summer by Flt Lt James Lindsay, who shot down four Bf 109s in it, including three in one sortie (*Canadian Forces*)

This was James Lindsay's first victory, and he was to become an ace before the summer was out. Post-war, he was the most successful Commonwealth pilot in the Korean War when, flying F-86 Sabres with the USAF's 51st Fighter Wing, he claimed two MiG-15s destroyed and three more damaged in 1952.

## LOSSES TO FLAK

On 12 May 2nd TAF underwent a reorganisation, part of which involved the creation of 'Wings' from the previous 'Airfields'. In preparation for the invasion, the three Canadian Spitfire squadrons of the newly re-titled No 144 Wing had moved under canvas to Ford, on the south coast, from where, on 15 May, 'Johnnie' Johnson led an escort for B-26s in somewhat indifferent weather. The Wing was also tasked with fighter-bomber work against 'Noball' (V1) targets. Thus, for all 2nd TAF Spitfire units, the daily round of strafing attacks continued, with most pilots now living under canvas at ALGs in southern England.

The ADGB units also flew offensively. For example, on 14 May eight Spitfires of Nos 1 and 165 Sqns at Predannack undertook an early morning 'Instep'. Later that same day No 1 Sqn CO Sqn Ldr Pat Lardner-Burke, flying Spitfire IX ML119/JX-B, led a 'Rodeo' (a fighter sweep over enemy territory) to Vannes looking for German bombers that had been reported on an airfield in the area. Although they found nothing, the Spitfire pilots strafed Gael airfield and a passing train. These attacks continued to take a heavy toll on the squadrons, however.

The Czech-manned No 312 Sqn was initially part of 2nd TAF, and in May 1944 it was based at Appledram ALG in Kent. Spitfire IX MJ631/DU-L is seen at the airfield marked with the Czech roundel and unit badge near the cockpit (*Zdenek Hurt*)

During a 'Ranger' (freelance flights over enemy territory by units of any size, their intention being to occupy and tire enemy fighters) to Dreux on the afternoon of the 18th eight-victory Polish ace Flg Off Mieczyslaw Adamek was hit by flak over Fecamp. Although he successfully bailed out off Beachy Head, he drowned. Then, on the evening of 19 May, No 411 Sqn's ace CO Sqn Ldr Norm Fowlow was

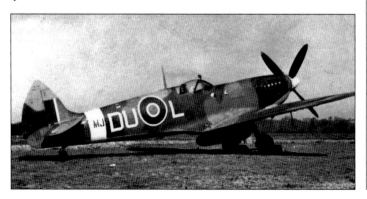

Pilots from No 485 (New Zealand) Sqn relax outside their tent at Selsey just before D-Day. Standing on the left is six-victory ace Flt Lt Owen Hardy and seated, smoking his pipe, is the CO, Sqn Ldr John Niven, who also had a number of aerial victories to his name (*RNZAF*)

leading a dive-bombing attack on a railway crossing at Hazebrouck when, over the target, flak hit and detonated the 500-lb bomb he was carrying. Although Fowlow managed to bail out of his shattered Spitfire IX, he did not survive. Flt Lt Graham Robertson was promoted and took command, noting that 'the squadron was hanging on a split yarn in anticipation of the invasion'.

The concerted Allied offensive against the enemy transport system continued on 21 May when 2nd TAF Spitfire squadrons flew a series of attacks, but with disastrous results as no fewer than 16 fighters were lost to flak during the course of the day. What was grimly called 'The Big Chop' resulted in the loss of several aces, including No 66 Sqn's CO Sqn Ldr Keith Lofts, who went down north of Bayeux but evaded capture. No 303 Sqn's Flt Lt Stanislaw Brzeski was less fortunate, however, for he became a PoW after he was shot down over the Pas de Calais. Flt Lt Josek Jeka of No 308 Sqn, who crash-landed near Buchy, also evaded capture, as did the CO of No 310 (Czech) Sqn, Sqn Ldr Hugo Hrbacek.

21 May also saw No 274 Sqn make its debut when Sqn Ldr Eddie Edwards, in BS227 (his regular aircraft), led it on a Wing sweep to the Berck-sur-Mer-Beaumont area. By the end of the month the newcomers had flown 125 operational sorties. The next day No 416 Sqn sent out a series of 'Rangers' and at last found some aerial action, with Flt Lts Richard Forbes-Roberts and George Patterson each shooting down an Fw 190 near Vernon. The latter pilot described the first of his three victories as follows;

'I saw an Fw 190 about 500 ft below and immediately attacked, opening fire at about 400 yards at about 15 degrees. Then this Focke-Wulf straightened out as my cannon stopped. I closed to about 50 yards line

On 27 April 1944 No 132 Sqn's CO, Sqn Ldr Geoffrey Page (second from left), discusses the first Spitfire escort into Germany with his pilots at Ford. This mission had been carried out the previous day, Spitfires covering heavy bombers that hit targets between Aachen and Cologne. The mission had been a personal success for Page, who had shared in the destruction of a Junkers W 34 transport southeast of Cologne for his seventh success. He was to more than double his tally of victories by the end of the summer (*P H T Green Collection*)

On the eve of D-Day groundcrew from No 411 Sqn paint the distinctive black and white AEAF identification stripes onto a Spitfire IX by hand at Tangmere (*DND*)

astern with machine guns, and his belly tank blew up. He struck the ground and burned. During my attack I saw a single-engined aircraft spinning about 500 yards to my left at about 500 ft.'

In all No 416 Sqn claimed five destroyed on 22 May. Two days later No 401 Sqn's CO, Sqn Ldr Lorne Cameron, moved to the verge of acedom when, providing top cover to bombers attacking Lille, he spotted a Focke-Wulf at low level and dived down to despatch it.

Escorts, sweeps and dive-bombing attacks continued unabated as June dawned. For example, Australian-manned No 453 Sqn was led by its ace CO Sqn Ldr Don Smith in an attack on rail targets at Hazebrouck and 'Noball' sites in the Pas de Calais. Sqn Ldr Geoffrey Page's No 132 Sqn also targeted V1 launch platforms, these missions often being led by future ace Flt Lt Mike Graham. Further west, Sqn Ldr Pat Lardner-Burke's No 1 Sqn flew its first bombing attack against shipping in Brest during the first week of June.

On the evening of 5 June ADGB had a total of 22 Merlin-engined Spitfire squadrons equipped with 424 aircraft, whilst in 2nd TAF there were a further 27 squadrons and 480 aircraft split between nine Wings. A start was made at this time to hastily paint broad black and white Allied Expeditionary Air Force (AEAF) identity stripes onto each and every Spitfire.

The main task for ADGB before and immediately after D-Day was to protect the assembling invasion fleet from the prying eyes of Luftwaffe reconnaissance aircraft. This mission mainly fell to the high-altitude Spitfire VIIs, and in the early days of June Nos 131 and 616 Sqns flew patrols providing top cover to the mass of shipping assembled in Lyme Bay and off Portland, for example. From Bradwell Bay No 124 Sqn flew similar patrols over the Dover Strait, such as that flown by future ace Flt Lt Peter Ayerst who, in early June logged daily patrols in Spitfire VII EN497/ON-P between Dungeness and North Foreland, including three on the 5th.

That night at Tangmere at 2330 hrs Gp Capt W R 'Iron Bill' MacBrien, commanding No 126 Wing, told his assembled squadrons, 'This is it!'

# NORMANDY

At last, the waiting was over! Throughout the previous day Spitfires had helped protect the massive assembly of shipping during its sea passage, a task then continued by the nightfighters. Through the early hours of 6 June Allied airborne forces had landed by parachute and glider and Royal Marine Commandos had scaled cliffs to secure key objectives and neutralise enemy strong points along the coast of Normandy. And then as dawn broke the seaborne landings began on five beaches, codenamed *Gold, Juno, Sword, Utah* and *Omaha*. The latter two were American and formed the western assault area, the other three were part of the eastern assault area for the Anglo-Canadian 21st Army Group. The initial cover from sunrise was provided by ADGB squadrons, with No 11 Group being responsible for fighter cover over the beachhead during the assault phase.

On 6 June – D-Day – all nightfighters were ordered to be clear of the Normandy assault area by 0430 hrs to allow the day fighters to take over responsibility, and through the day these aircraft flew more than 1500 sorties, nearly 900 of them by Spitfires. The fighters patrolled continuously at medium level, or below cloud, over all five beaches and inland to a depth of five miles. They also covered the vast assault fleet offshore, each squadron undertaking 50-minute low patrols.

First over the area were the Spitfire VBs of Nos 130, 501 and 611 Sqns, a patrol from the Wing having taken off from Harrowbeer at 0350 hrs under the leadership of ace Wg Cdr Peter Powell. It overflew *Omaha* and *Gold* beaches before returning shortly after 0600 hrs, the Wing's aircraft having been the first ADGB fighters to witness the landings. After a hasty breakfast, pilots from all three squadrons were soon airborne on another patrol. Remarkably, No 501's Spitfire VB X4272/SD-J, flown that morning by Flt Lt J R Davies, had participated in the Battle of Britain! Also flying with No 501 Sqn was Flt Lt Warren Peglar, who described the scene to the author;

'On the morning of 6 June I was sent on patrol, leading a flight of four Spitfires over *Juno* and *Sword* beaches. We were airborne at first light and the sight was absolutely awesome. We had become accustomed to flying over a vast and empty Channel, which was now filled with hundreds of ships, ploughing through some nasty, rainy weather and fairly heavy seas. When we arrived over the beachhead, and took up our patrol station, it seemed to be an orderly, even easy, invasion – this being observed from 10,000 ft. Little did we realise what an awful battle was taking place down there. We flew over the east flank of the invasion again in the afternoon of D-Day and, again, did not see much action below, aside from the massive fleet just off the beaches.'

Pairs of Spitfire VIIs from Nos 131 and 124 Sqns flew high-altitude patrols from 0515 hrs, Flt Lt Peter Ayerst from the latter unit, who flew in EN497/ON-P, noting in his logbook 'D-Day – very quiet'! 2nd TAF Spitfires were also active of course, Sqn Ldr Geoffrey Page, in MK144/FF-O, leading No 132 Sqn over *Utah* beach at 0800 hrs. Others in this

patrol included future aces Flt Lt Mike Graham in FF-Y and WO Desmond Watkins in MJ784/FF-C. The units made further patrols into the evening. Most missions were uneventful, No 411 Sqn, for example, patrolling the eastern beaches from 0810 hrs without seeing any action. The D-Day experience of future ace Flt Lt Bob Hayward was typical, for he flew four sorties with No 411 Sqn on 6 June and did not see a single enemy aircraft. Indeed, the day's activities led the unit diarist to comment, 'This was very disappointing'.

In 'Johnnie' Johnson's No 144 Wing, No 442 Sqn's activities during D-Day mirrored those of many other units. The pilots were woken at 0315 hrs and the squadron mounted its first patrol at 0630 hrs. When the last aircraft touched down at 2200 hrs No 442 Sqn had flown 94 hours during the course of four patrols. Each had been led by the CO, Dal Russel, the diary noting that pilots had witnessed 'scenes that were indelibly impressed on their memories – the Channel covered with shipping, fighting on the beaches, gliders landing and battles between Allied and enemy tanks'. In No 441 Sqn Flt Lt Freddie Wilson was hit by flak during a low cover patrol and forced to crash-land at Ford.

No 453 Sqn was also up early, flying its first patrol over the beachhead from 0800 hrs with Sqn Ldr Don Smith in the vanguard in Spitfire IX MH487/FU-J. This proved to be an uneventful mission, save for seeing the US Navy destroyer USS *Corry* (DD-463) sinking off Îles Saint-Marcouf after it had been struck by rounds from a German shore battery. In an interview at the time with an Australian journalist Smith said;

'We knew it was on when we went on patrol on the evening of 5 June. We saw the greatest convoy the world had ever known. And when we got back to base in England we attended a memorable mass briefing, where we learned the details of the tremendous invasion plan. On D-Day we were out patrolling the coast and the Allied beachhead. We were sightseers. We saw this great battle begin. As the invasion fleet approached the enemy coast I watched Bomber Command's heavies go into action. High on the cliff of a small headland there was a battery of heavy German guns – six

On the morning of 6 June 1944, the CO of No 453 Sqn, Sqn Ldr Don Smith, flew over the Normandy beaches in Spitfire IX NH487/FU-J (seen here furthest from the camera) as his usual FU-? was unserviceable. Before landing back at 1015 hrs, he had seen the US Navy destroyer USS *Corry* (DD-463) sinking off Îles Saint-Marcouf after it had been struck by rounds from a German shore battery (*RAAF*)

When New Zealander Flg Off Johnny Houlton of No 485 Sqn shot down a Ju 88 on the afternoon of 6 June 1944 it was credited to him as the first aerial victory claimed since the start of the D-Day invasion (*J A Houlton*)

or eight of them in a great concrete emplacement. That battery was completely wiped out. I have seen some good bombing since the war began, but nothing to equal this.'

By dusk No 453 Sqn had flown 43 sorties.

From the far west of England No 1 Sqn flew 30 sorties on 'Roadstead' (dive-bombing and low level attacks on enemy ships at sea or in harbour) patrols, helping to seal off the western Channel from any possible interference by the Kriegsmarine.

Whilst there was initially little sign of the Luftwaffe, at about 1545 hrs the RNZAF's No 485 Sqn spotted some Ju 88s. These were not bombers, however, but Ju 88C long-range fighters of I./ZG 1 that had been despatched from Brittany. With No 222 Sqn flying as top cover, No 485 Sqn went down after the enemy aircraft, as future ace Flg Off Johnny Houlton (flying Spitfire IX MK950/OU-X) described in his autobiography;

'In mid-afternoon I led Blue Section during the third patrol of the day. South of *Omaha* beach, below a shallow, broken layer of cumulus, I glimpsed a Ju 88 above cloud, diving away fast to the south. Climbing at full throttle, I saw the enemy aircraft enter a large isolated cloud above the main layer, and when it reappeared on the other side I was closing in rapidly.

'I adjusted the gyro gunsight onto the target at 500 yards, with a deflection angle of 45 degrees, positioned the aiming dot on the right-hand engine of the enemy aircraft and fired a three-second burst. The engine disintegrated, fire broke out, two crewmen bailed out and the aircraft dived steeply to crash on a roadway, blowing apart on impact. As I turned back towards the beachhead I sighted a second Ju 88 heading south, so I made an almost identical attack, which stopped the right hand engine. The aircraft then went into a steep, jinking dive, with the rear gunner firing at other members of my section who all attacked, until the Ju 88 flattened out and crash-landed at high speed. One of its propellers broke free, spinning and bounding far away across the fields and hedges like a giant Catherine wheel.

'Supreme Headquarters nominated the first Ju 88 I had destroyed as the first enemy aircraft to be shot down since the invasion began, putting No 485 (NZ) Spitfire Squadron at the top of the scoreboard for D-Day.'

A few minutes later No 349 Sqn – No 485 Sqn's Belgian colleagues in No 135 Wing – shot down two more Ju 88s and damaged a further four, one of the latter being amongst the six claims of Flt Lt Gaby Seydel. Sadly, during an earlier patrol by their countrymen of No 350 Sqn, Spitfire VB EN950/MN-H flown by Belgian ace Flt Lt Francois Venesoen had suffered a serious glycol leak in flight. Although Venesoen bailed out off Friston he drowned, thus becoming the first ace to be lost in a Spitfire after the invasion had commenced.

Patrols by Spitfire units continued into the night, with, amongst others, No 234 Sqn (including Malta ace Flt Lt 'Wally' Walton) escorting Dakotas and Horsas flying reinforcements in to the airborne troops as part of Operation *Mallard*.

During what became known as the Longest Day, there had been remarkably little reaction from the Luftwaffe, but that was to change during the coming days and weeks.

## INVASION ACES

The Luftwaffe reaction to the invasion began in earnest on 7 June when, during some hectic action over Normandy, 34 enemy aircraft were claimed shot down, almost half falling to Spitfires. No 401 Sqn was over *Gold* beach early, as its diarist recorded;

'At least a dozen Ju 88s suddenly appeared out of cloud, some managing to dive at the beaches, the rest turning as we attacked and attempting to reach cloud. Sqn Ldr Cameron called on everyone to pick his own target, and the squadron broke up.'

One fell to the No 126 Wing Leader, Wg Cdr George Keefer, in Spitfire IX MK826/GCK, whose fifth victory made him the first Spitfire pilot to reach acedom since the invasion;

'I was leading No 412 Sqn at 6000 ft over *Sword* beach when ack-ack started firing behind and above us. We broke around to port and then saw several Hun bombers below us to the west just above cloud at 3000 ft. I told everyone to get into them. I picked one nipping in and out of cloud and gave him two short bursts from the port quarter. It caught fire and blew up, with one engine flying off after the explosion. One person bailed out from the Ju 88.'

A few minutes later two more fell to Lorne Cameron, making him an ace, whilst Flt Lt Phil Charron of No 412 Sqn (in Spitfire IX MJ485), who had gained two victories over Malta in 1942, also shot down a Ju 88 to claim his third success. Thirty minutes later, Keefer's opposite number in the Free French No 145 Wing, Wg Cdr Bill Crawford-Compton, flying Spitfire IX 'WVC', shot down another Ju 88 to claim his 18th success.

During an early afternoon patrol, No 401 Sqn's Flg Off Bill Klersy, in Mk IX MJ289, shot down an Fw 190 to claim the first fighter destroyed by a Spitfire since the invasion. In the early evening his colleagues in No 411 Sqn also found action, unit CO Sqn Ldr Graham Robertson downing another Fw 190 to begin his path to acedom. Flt Lt George Johnson also destroyed a Focke-Wulf for the first of his eight victories, noting in his combat report;

'I went down with Red Leader on two enemy aircraft chasing a Thunderbolt on the deck. They split and I took the port one. My first burst from 600 yards dead astern knocked small pieces off. I then fired several bursts during a steep turn, without seeing results. The enemy aircraft straightened, and I noticed strikes on the cockpit and engine. Smoke poured from the enemy aircraft and it crashed into a farmhouse.'

The pre-eminence of the RCAF Spitfire squadrons during the Northwest Europe campaign was already beginning, although the RAF also joined the party. Amongst the latter units was No 501 Sqn, which was led over the beachhead at dawn on 8 June by No 142 Wing CO Wg Cdr Johnny Checketts. During the course of this mission the squadron gained its first victory since the invasion, the action being described as follows in the unit history;

Like most wing leaders, Wg Cdr George Keefer has his aircraft (Spitfire IX MK826) marked with his initials, GCK. Flying this machine in the weeks after D-Day, he shot down four aircraft to become the first pilot to become an ace after the invasion – he had previous victory claims from his time in North Africa in 1941-42. Keefer 'made ace' with the destruction of a Ju 88 on 7 June 1944 (*via C H Thomas*)

'The squadron was vectored to the scene of Luftwaffe activity. Changing course, more enemy aircraft were reported on the squadron's flank, so Yellow Section detached itself and spotted six Me 109s below them, heading away from Le Havre. Flt Lt "Foob" Fairbanks, the piano-playing American, tore into the enemy fighters, sending one down in flames and badly damaging another.'

These victories over Deauville were Fairbanks' only ones with the Spitfire, although he was to gain a further 11.5 victories when flying Tempest Vs to become the leading ace on that type. During No 501 Sqn's first successful combat of the year Flt Lt L P 'Griff' Griffith shot down a second Bf 109, whilst Checketts in his personally marked Spitfire VB AB509/JMC damaged a third.

This success continued during the course of the day, with No 485 Sqn spotting a formation of Bf 109s and Fw 190s when providing low cover over the canal at Ouistreham during the early evening. Flying Spitfire IX ML407/OU-V, No 485 Sqn's Johnnie Houlton shot down a Bf 109, as he described in his autobiography;

'I was leading Blue Section below cloud, flying straight at the canal from the east, and called for the section to make a steep climbing turn to the right up through the cloud layer. By sheer luck, three of us emerged behind a formation of 20 Me 109s and ahead of some pursuing Spitfires that were out of range. As we latched onto three of the tail-enders the whole German gaggle – which was flying in three sections in loose line astern – began porpoising in and out of another cloud layer above us. It was an unusual and frustrating sensation following these undulations, and trying to line up for a short burst each time the target briefly popped out of cloud.

'By my fourth attempt I was about 50 yards behind, and closing fast, as the Me 109 reappeared and pulled up again. This time I followed him into the cloud, firing a long burst as OU-V bounced around in his slipstream. Just as I heard Frank yell "I've got the bastard" over the R/T, a great blob of black smoke and debris came back at me through the murk, and I half-rolled to break cloud simultaneously with the Me 109, which was trailing smoke and diving for the deck. Two other Me 109s were going down in flames – one destroyed by Frank and the other by Pat – while the one I had hit started to flatten out of its dive just as it crashed in a wood.'

Thus had the New Zealander become the latest Spitfire ace.

Flying Spitfire IX ML407/OU-V over Normandy on 8 June, Flg Off Johnny Houlton shot down a Bf 109 to become an ace. Using the same fighter to destroy another Messerschmitt four days later, he continued to fly ML407 throughout the summer. Houlton is seen here at its controls during a bomber escort mission to the Ruhr on 27 August 1944 (*J A Houlton*)

On 9 June the weather intervened, restricting much of the Allied air activity to some defensive patrols over the beaches. In murky conditions ships' gunners tended to fire first, and the CO of No 331 Sqn, ace Maj Leif Lundsten, was shot down and killed by American ships off the coast near Isigny.

As the fighting on the ground against German opposition intensified, there was also an increase in aerial combat. Whilst losses, mainly due to flak, began to mount, so too did aerial combat claims. Indeed, on 10 June alone Allied (mainly USAAF) fighters claimed 33 German aircraft destroyed. The first RAF claim of the day came at around 0700 hrs when Flt Lt George Varley (who had previously flown catapult Hurricanes from merchant ships) of No 222 Sqn claimed the first of his four victories when he hit an Fw 190 over the beachhead and saw its pilot bail out. Late in the evening No 611 Sqn's CO, 23-year-old Scotsman Sqn Ldr Bill Douglas, was flying Mk VB BM345 near Saintenay when he shot down a Ju 88 to become the first ADGB Spitfire pilot to become an ace since the invasion. His wingman bagged a second Junkers bomber.

Douglas gave the following description of the action in his combat report, the pilot also highlighting the problems that day fighters faced when flying at night;

'Seeing bomb bursts and AA fire from Carentan, I proceeded to the south of this area at 5000 ft. I saw four twin-engined aircraft approaching in close formation from the south at 5000 ft. Seeing them silhouetted against a stretch of low cloud, I dived down beneath them and approached from below and astern, keeping myself against a dark background. I identified the aircraft as Ju 88s and closed in astern and below the rear starboard bomber. I pulled into dead astern at 70-100 yards and opened fire. As I did so the port Ju 88 opened fire on me. I observed strikes in the port mainplane and fuselage of the Ju 88 I was attacking and the enemy aircraft blew up. I felt something hit me, so I broke away to avoid colliding with it. I lost control for a few seconds, then looked round and saw the enemy aircraft going down in flames. It hit the ground about six miles south of Carentan and burned there. One of my exhaust blinkers was missing, and on landing I found the spinner dented and the mirror missing.'

Significantly, 10 June also saw Allied fighters using landing strips in the expanding beachhead for the first time, aircraft being refuelled and rearmed. Sqn Ldr Dal Russel and three others from No 442 Sqn landed at B3 Ste-Croix-sur-Mer, before returning to Ford at 1800 hrs. The next day No 453 Sqn's CO, Sqn Ldr Don Smith, led 12 Spitfires on a sweep over Normandy and landed at an ALG for an uncomfortable night's stay – a foretaste of what was to come when 2nd TAF moved to the Continent.

As dawn broke on 12 June, Flg Off Johnny Houlton, once more in Spitfire IX ML407/OU-V, spotted a pair of Bf 109s that he and his wingman, Flt Lt Bill Newenham, chased. Houlton hit his with an accurate burst and it blew up in mid air, while Newenham's victim crashed into a wood. Houlton commented that the pilot of his Bf 109 seemed to use an ejector system to escape from his fighter, but this was undoubtedly due to the violence of the explosion! These proved to be No 485 Sqn's last aerial victories of the war.

Spitfires flying with No 10 Group of ADGB wore much narrower AEAF stripes, as is evident on Spitfire IX MK989/5J-L of No 126 Sqn in which WO Hinton had fuel transfer problems on a patrol and had to force land at the USAAF base at Upottery on 19 June (*Charles H Young*)

At 1300 hrs that same day Wg Cdr Peter Brothers led his Spitfire VII-equipped Nos 131 and 616 Sqns from Culmhead on a sweep over southern Normandy, strafing the airfields at Le Mans and Laval. Over the former, Flt Lt Vincent 'Junior' Moody from No 131 Sqn went down, having probably fallen victim to flak. Near Laval the squadrons became embroiled with Bf 109s, probably from Hauptmann Rudolf Sinner's I./JG 27, and Fw 190s of I./JG 11. In the ensuing action five were claimed destroyed, two Fw 190s falling to Flt Lt Jack Clelland from No 616 Sqn, who wrote in his log book, 'MB768/YQ-X. Destroyed two FW 190s. Hit by flak in wing, hood and engine. Bailed out 12 miles southwest of Portland Bill. Picked up by ASR [Air-Sea Rescue] launch 15 minutes later'.

The wingtip of another No 616 Sqn aircraft, flown by Flt Lt Harrison, struck a Bf 109 and took its tail off, sending it down. As Harrison called that he was going to bail out, his aircraft (MD121) dived suddenly from 1000 ft before he could do so, killing him in the resulting crash. Geoffrey Harrison had become an ace just moments before his death.

During the evening two Spitfire VIIs from No 124 Sqn – MD164/ON-P flown by Flt Lt Peter Ayerst and MD139/ON-W flown by Flg Off 'Jesse' Hibbert – scrambled from Bradwell Bay and, off the North Foreland, shot down a Bf 109. Ayerst wrote in his logbook, 'Patrol Gris Nez – North Foreland. Destroyed a Me 109G with Flt Lt Hibbert 20 miles east of North Foreland. Pilot bailed out. Saw Air-Sea Rescue launches looking for Hun pilot'. He also recounted this action to the author many years later;

'We were scrambled high over the Channel, and I recall that the weather was pretty "thick". In the cloud we finally spotted this Jerry '109, probably on a recce as it was just after the invasion. We managed to get closer to him, probably helped by the light grey camouflage our Spits had, as we were a "special" high-altitude squadron. I managed to get in several squirts at him that hit all over his wing before he disappeared into the murk. We floundered about for a bit following directions from control before my No 2 spotted him and put in some further bursts, and down he went and he bailed out.'

Their victim was probably a strategic reconnaissance aircraft from *Fernnaufklarungsgruppe Oberkommando der Luftwaffe*, the share in the Bf 109's demise elevating Peter Ayerst to ace status and giving 'Jesse' Hibbert his second victory – he too later became an ace while flying Tempest Vs.

Fully bedecked in AEAF stripes, Spitfire IX NH171/AH-Z of No 332 Sqn awaits its next sortie over the beaches from Bognor. It wears Norwegian colours around the spinner (*Nils Mathisrud*)

Peter Ayerst was a fan of the Spitfire VII, noting 'I enjoyed flying it at high altitude. We had a new Merlin 64 engine fitted with a two-speed two-stage supercharger, thus giving the aircraft a far better performance at height. But the incessant high-altitude sorties that we flew over the Channel were exhausting'.

Sadly, 2nd TAF suffered a severe loss the next day (13 June) when, to the northeast of Caen, the No 127 Wing Leader, Canadian ace Wg Cdr Lloyd Chadburn, flying his Spitfire IX MJ824/LVC, collided with his wingman and both pilots were killed.

As Allied troops struggled to achieve the breakthrough that was not to come for many more long, bloody, weeks, so the air fighting intensified over the wider battle area, leading to a steady rise in claims and casualties. Flying from Detling on 14 June, No 80 Sqn, under the leadership of Norwegian ace Maj Bjorn Bjornstad, had a brief fight. Several hours later, over *Omaha* beach, a patrol from No 611 Sqn spotted 16 Bf 109s in tight formation just below the cloud base. The resulting attack ended with four German fighters being claimed as destroyed. One of these was credited to the CO, Sqn Ldr Bill Douglas, as his sixth victory, leading him to remark 'What a party!' upon returning to Harrowbeer.

Early on 15 June Lt Col Rolf Berg led No 132 Wing on a sweep, and at 10,000 ft over Evreux engaged some 20 Fw 190s and Bf 109s. Eight German fighters were claimed shot down, including one by No 332 Sqn's CO, Maj Werner Christie, for his sixth victory.

His opposite number in No 66 Sqn, Sqn Ldr Tim Johnston, also got an Fw 190 to take his total to five and one shared, whilst the Fw 190 claimed by No 331 Sqn's 2Lt Ragnar Dogger was his fourth victory. Later that day Free French pilot Asp Pierre Clostermann also claimed his fourth victory.

On 17 June No 611 Sqn's Free French ace Lt Robert Gouby, flying Spitfire VB BL472, shot down an Fw 190 near Penniers to claim his ninth, and last, success. The 24-year-old subsequently fell to flak while strafing a convoy near Guigles on 14 August.

Czech pilot Flt Lt Otto Smik became an ace during 1943, and whilst serving with No 310 Sqn in June-July 1944 he claimed three more victories to take his score to ten. Smik routinely flew Spitfire IX MJ291/NN-N, on which he is seated, that also displays his scoreboard (*Zdenek Hurt*)

The evening prior to Gouby's last victory, Sqn Ldr Wally McLeod's No 443 Sqn was in action once more when, just south of Caen, it became embroiled in a whirling dogfight. McLeod, in Spitfire IX 2I-E, shot down a Bf 109 and Wg Cdr 'Johnnie' Johnson claimed an Fw 190. The latter pilot noted in his combat report, 'I dived and opened fire on the starboard enemy aircraft, which was slightly behind the other three. Strikes were seen on the engine cowling and cockpit of the enemy aircraft, which dived into the ground and disintegrated'. However, accurate light flak shot down four aircraft in what was a bad day for No 443 Sqn. On 18 June Wg Cdr Johnson was awarded a second bar to his DSO.

Exiled pilots were also in action over France, including Flg Off Otto Smik of No 310 Sqn, flying Spitfire IX MJ291/NN-N, who, during the evening of 17 June, shot down an Fw 190 southeast of Caen and shared in the destruction of a second fighter. Smik's last victories took his total to eight and two shared. Three days later, an early patrol from No 331 Sqn shot down a Bf 109 near Douvres. A share in this victory made Capt Nils Jörstad the latest Norwegian ace.

On 22 June No 442 Sqn finally claimed its first victories following action near Argentan. Returning from a sweep led by 'Johnnie' Johnson, the unit spotted Bf 109s and Fw 190s 7000 ft below. Diving down, they destroyed four of them – Johnson claimed one and the CO, Sqn Ldr Dal Russel, was credited with his first success in almost four years when he shared the destruction of an Fw 190 with Flt Lt John Marriot.

Shortly before midday on the 23rd four fighters from Nos 132 and 602 Sqns took on more than 12 German fighters south of Caen directly over the heads of Allied troops. No 132 Sqn's CO, Sqn Ldr Geoffrey Page (in Spitfire IX MK144/FF-O), claimed his ninth victory when he shot down an Fw 190, as he described in his book;

'Taking a steady deflection at an estimated 300 yards range, I pressed the firing button for two seconds. The chug of the cannons and the chatter of the machine guns filled the cockpit with distant noise. Ahead, a column of brown smoke appeared from the German as he peeled away gently from his formation, which flew on still ignorant of the presence of RAF fighters. Perplexed at the behaviour of my target I closed to within 100 yards and fired again. Pieces of metal flew off the FW 190, but still it continued on its steady gentle dive towards the battlefields below.'

The following day Page located the wreck and claimed the swastika-covered fin as a prize for his squadron!

Later in the afternoon of 23 June a patrol of five Spitfires from No 403 Sqn encountered 15 *Jabo* Fw 190s northeast of Caen, one of which Flt Lt 'Mac' Gordon in Spitfire IX MK730 shot down to begin his path to acedom, whilst in the evening McLeod's No 443 Sqn was again engaged. Superb gunnery saw the Canadian expend just 50 cannon rounds whilst shooting down two enemy fighters;

'I fired from 75 yards at a Fw 190. Strikes observed. He went down through cloud. I followed, firing another short burst. The port wing came off and the aircraft crashed half a mile north of Alençon. I next observed an Fw 190 below cloud. I followed, and it rolled onto its back and went straight in a quarter of a mile from the first.'

Preventing the Luftwaffe from attacking the slowly expanding beachhead or the shipping offshore was a vital task for the fighter squadrons, but for most of the tactical units, armed reconnaissance and ground attacks predominated through into July.

By the end of June several more Spitfire pilots had become aces over the Normandy battlefield. On the 26th Sous-Lt Pierre Clostermann of No 602 Sqn was scrambled from B11 Longues (the unit had flown in just 24 hours earlier) and sent after enemy fighters seen flying near Caen. As he passed over the river Orne he engaged four Fw 190s and destroyed one of them near Carpiquet airfield to became the latest Free French ace. The following afternoon Wg Cdr George Keefer of No 126 Wing, in Spitfire IX MK826/GCK, was scrambled from B4 Bény-sur-Mer. As he neared Beaumont-le-Roger Keefer intercepted 12+ Bf 109s, one of which he shot down to claim his eighth victory, and last with a Merlin-engined Spitfire.

28 June would prove to be the high point of the aerial fighting over Normandy, with 34 enemy aircraft destroyed (26 of them by the RCAF) in more than a dozen engagements as the Luftwaffe attempted to support a great tank battle raging around Caen.

That day Wg Cdr 'Johnnie' Johnson, flying his personal Spitfire IX MK392/JEJ, led No 442 Sqn on an armed reconnaissance. As the aircraft neared Villers-Bocage they intercepted Bf 109 fighter-bombers and Johnson swiftly destroyed two of them. Flg Off Larry Robillard, in Mk IX MK777/Y2-Z, shot down another Bf 109 to at last become an ace, as he subsequently described in his combat report;

'We saw seven '109s with bombs coming head-on. They were flying in two sections. I was closest to the '109s and pulled around on the last one, who jettisoned his bomb. I gave one squirt at about 200 yards, no strikes seen, then allowed a little less deflection and his port tailplane blew off with numerous strikes. I pulled through a bit more and saw strikes along his fuselage and engine. There was a flash of flame followed by thick smoke and the aircraft went down in flames, apparently out of control.'

Two hours later No 411 Sqn had a fight 20 miles south of Le Havre, during which Flt Lt Hugh Trainor shot down a Bf 109 to begin his path to acedom. No 411 was airborne again at about 2000 hrs, when, near Caen, Trainor shot down an Fw 190, as did Flt Lt George Johnson for the second of his eight victories. Finally, squadronmate, and

Resplendent with its No 602 Sqn badge on the nose, Spitfire IX MJ586/LO-D was the mount of Free French ace Sous-Lt Pierre Clostermann. His impressive personal score can just be seen under the cockpit. Flying it on 29 June, he claimed his sixth victory when he shot down an Fw 190 near Rouen (*P H Clostermann via C H Thomas*)

A pair of Spitfire IXs from No 442 Sqn, MK464/Y2-Y leads MK777/Y2-Z into the air as they scramble from B4 Beny-sur-Mer in early August. Flying the latter machine on 27 June 1944, ace Flt Lt Harry Dowding had shot down a pair of Bf 109s for his final victories. The following morning future ace Flg Off Larry Robillard destroyed another Messerschmitt with this aircraft (*Donald Nijboer*)

Newfoundlander, Flt Lt Bob Hayward bagged a brace of Focke-Wulfs to become an ace. A little earlier in the day No 421 Sqn had been credited with two Bf 109s when Flg Off John McElroy claimed his 11th victory and Flt Lt Hank Zary began his path to acedom.

The last action of 28 June involved No 401 Sqn, which had been strafing vehicles when it was bounced from out of the sun by 12 Fw 190s. In the ensuing dogfight four German fighters were destroyed, including two by Flg Off Bill Klersy. Another became the first success over Normandy for Flt Lt Irving 'Hap' Kennedy (flying Spitfire IX NH260/ YO-W), who already had 13 victories to his name from the Mediterranean. He wrote in his autobiography;

'A good old-fashioned scrap followed right down to ground level. My new Spit IX was too much for a Focke-Wulf pilot, who stayed around for the scrap. He had a good aircraft, but could not turn with a Spit IX, and when I got on his tail I knew I had him. One short burst and he was in the trees with a great flash of fire.'

The Free French units also regularly engaged in action over their homeland as improving weather continued to allow increased air support to blunt a strong German counter attack that had been launched on the VIII Corps front. On a wing sweep over Evreux the Free French No 145 Wing, led by Wg Cdr Bill Crawford-Crompton, hit eight German fighters near Beaumont-le-Roger, two of which fell to the New Zealand ace's guns for his penultimate successes. Lt Guignard of No 340 Sqn claimed another.

June ended with another successful day for the Spitfire units, which claimed 21 fighters shot down. At 0705 hrs No 421 Sqn was out early on a scramble, and Flt Lts Paul Johnson and Roger Wilson each shot down a Bf 109. Having achieved his third victory earlier in the day, the 24-year-old Johnson was in action again during the evening when, just to the east of Lisieux, he shot down a brace of Bf 109s to become an ace. Sadly, when strafing on 17 July, Johnson's aircraft hit a tree and he crashed to his death.

Other aces and future aces also made claims on 30 June during what proved to be yet another bad day for the Luftwaffe. 'Johnnie' Johnson, leading No 441 Sqn, shot down a Bf 109, as did Flt Lt Guy Mott to begin the path to acedom – a status that he was to achieve in less than a month;

'One Me 109 broke starboard and I followed him around in his break, on his tail. He levelled out and at approximately 300-400 yards I fired a four-second burst. I noticed cannon strikes on the wing and fuselage of the Me 109. He rolled over onto his back as I was still firing, and smoke and flame was coming from his belly. He then went straight into the ground.'

No 442 Sqn also made several claims, including a third victory for Flt Lt Dean Dover.

Flying from England, HQ Fighter Command staff officer, and ace, Wg Cdr Don Kingaby saw action in his personal Spitfire VB DEK when he joined a patrol of No 501 Sqn fighters. Kingaby and Flg Off Bob Stockburn shared in the destruction of a Bf 109 near Cazelle, this success being the ace's final claim and also No 501 Sqn's last Spitfire victory.

Late in the evening No 145 Wing covered a large force of Bomber Command 'heavies' attacking German armour at Villers-Bocage. No 341 Sqn shot down two Bf 109s that attempted to engage the bombers, one being claimed by Cne 'Jaco' Andrieux, making him an ace.

Shortly after claiming his final victories to take his total to eight, Harry Dowding was promoted to command No 442 Sqn (*DND*)

By the end of June 1944 the four Spitfire wings of No 83 Group had all moved into nine strips within the beachhead, although four of these were still within range of German artillery! The wings of No 84 Group remained in southern England for the time being, however, and they would fly more bomber escort missions during July. As June ended more than 875,000 Allied troops had been landed in Normandy, but in a month of bitter fighting they had suffered over 60,000 casualties.

## PREPARING FOR BREAKOUT

In contrast to previous days 1 July was much quieter, the only confirmed victory falling to No 132 Sqn's Sqn Ldr Geoffrey Page (again flying MK144/FF-O), who shared an Fw 190 when bounced whilst strafing motor transport southeast of Caen. Action exploded once more the following day, however, when 25 German fighters fell to Spitfires – 21 of them to the Canadians, four of whom became aces in the process.

No 411 Sqn was the first aloft on a dawn patrol, its pilots spotting four Fw 190s south of Caen. In a brief fight Flt Lt Esli Lapp opened his account when he destroyed the aircraft of Unteroffizier Gerhard Kraft of II./JG 26 who was killed. Lapp's wingman, WO Jeffrey, was shot down during the melee, although he evaded capture. Just after midday No 412 Sqn was in action, shooting down four Fw 190s. One of these made CO Sqn Ldr Jack Shepard an ace, two more fell to Flg Off Don Laubman and the final fighter was credited to Plt Off David Jamieson, who began his path to acedom. At the same time No 441 Sqn was up in sections of four, and near Lisieux it achieved a perfect 'bounce' on eight fighters. Flt Lt Leslie Moore (in Spitfire IX ML269) shot down two Bf 109s and shared in the destruction of a third. The first pilot from his squadron to become an ace following these victories, his combat report read as follows;

'I first attacked a Me 109, seeing strikes on him before breaking off the attack and watching the fighter crash in flames. I then attacked another Me 109, and I saw him gliding, streaming glycol, then crash into some woods. After climbing to about 2000 ft I saw a Spitfire break off an attack on another Me 109, which I then went after, seeing strikes on the engine cowling and cockpit. He slowed up and began losing height rapidly, and upon crashing burst into flames.' *(text continues on page 45)*

**With 16 victories claimed between March and October 1944, 22-year-old Flt Lt Don Laubman of No 412 Sqn became the most successful Spitfire pilot in 2nd TAF. Following a period of rest, he returned to operations in April 1945, only to be shot down by flak and briefly made a PoW (*DND*)**

**For most of his time with No 412 Sqn Flt Lt Don Laubman flew VZ-Z, the aircraft being seen here parked alongside a Typhoon on a Normandy ALG in July 1944 (*RCAF*)**

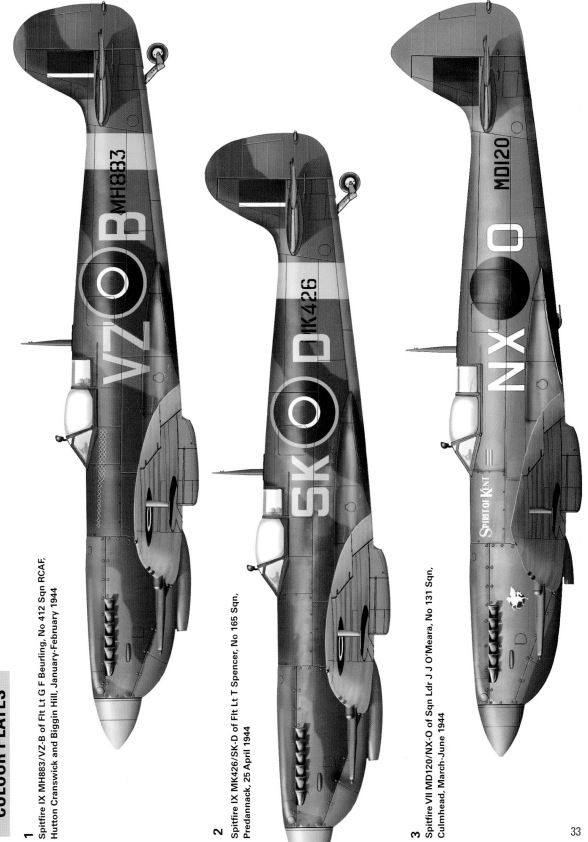

**1**
Spitfire IX MH883/VZ-B of Flt Lt G F Beurling, No 412 Sqn RCAF,
Hutton Cranswick and Biggin Hill, January-February 1944

**2**
Spitfire IX MK426/SK-D of Flt Lt T Spencer, No 165 Sqn,
Predannack, 25 April 1944

**3**
Spitfire VII MD120/NX-O of Sqn Ldr J J O'Meara, No 131 Sqn,
Culmhead, March–June 1944

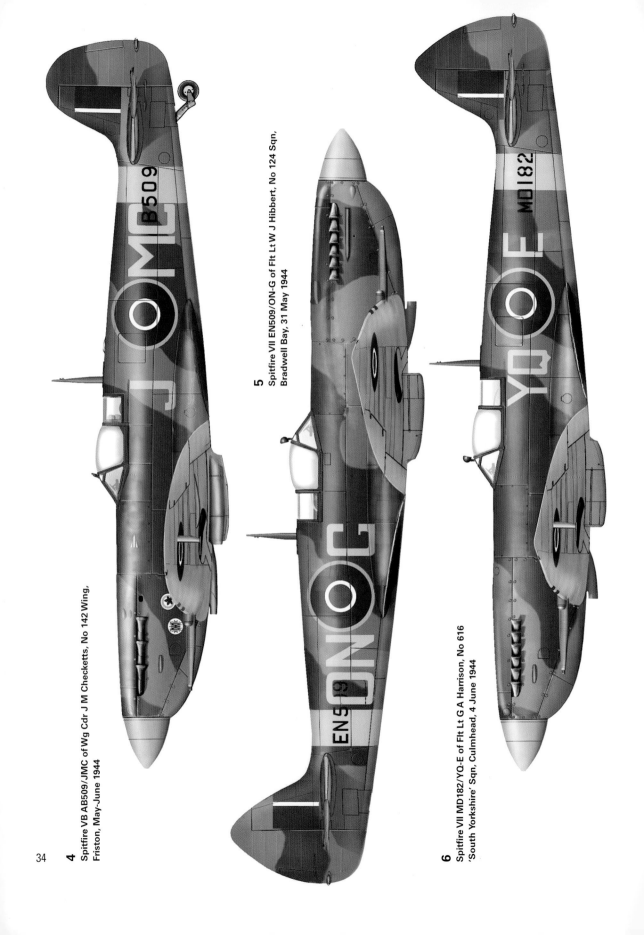

**4**
Spitfire VB AB509/JMC of Wg Cdr J M Checketts, No 142 Wing,
Friston, May-June 1944

**5**
Spitfire VII EN509/ON-G of Flt Lt W J Hibbert, No 124 Sqn,
Bradwell Bay, 31 May 1944

**6**
Spitfire VII MD182/YQ-E of Flt Lt G A Harrison, No 616
'South Yorkshire' Sqn, Culmhead, 4 June 1944

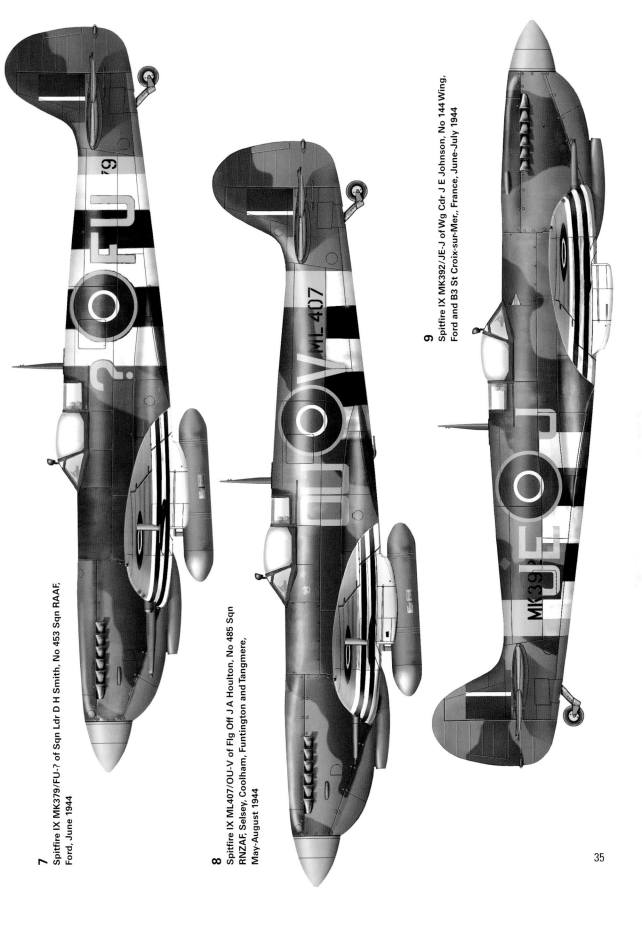

**7**
Spitfire IX MK379/FU-? of Sqn Ldr D H Smith, No 453 Sqn RAAF,
Ford, June 1944

**8**
Spitfire IX ML407/OU-V of Flg Off J A Houlton, No 485 Sqn
RNZAF, Selsey, Coolham, Funtington and Tangmere,
May-August 1944

**9**
Spitfire IX MK392/JE-J of Wg Cdr J E Johnson, No 144 Wing,
Ford and B3 St Croix-sur-Mer,, France, June-July 1944

35

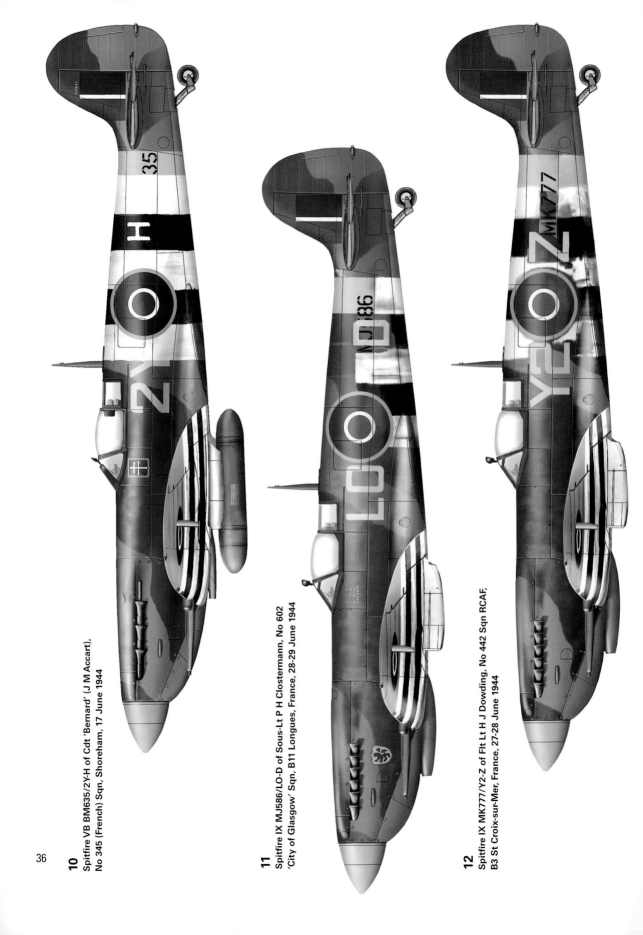

**10**
Spitfire VB BM635/2Y-H of Cdt 'Bernard' (J M Accart),
No 345 (French) Sqn, Shoreham, 17 June 1944

**11**
Spitfire IX MJ586/LO-D of Sous-Lt P H Clostermann, No 602
'City of Glasgow' Sqn, B11 Longues, France, 28-29 June 1944

**12**
Spitfire IX MK777/Y2-Z of Flt Lt H J Dowding, No 442 Sqn RCAF,
B3 St Croix-sur-Mer, France, 27-28 June 1944

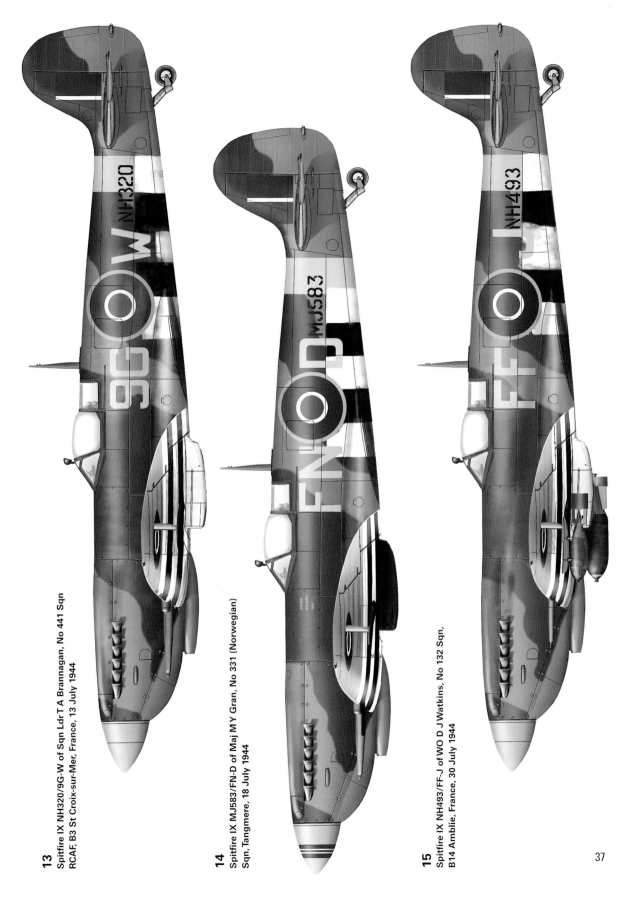

**13**
Spitfire IX NH320/9G-W of Sqn Ldr T A Brannagan, No 441 Sqn
RCAF, B3 St Croix-sur-Mer, France, 13 July 1944

**14**
Spitfire IX MJ583/FN-D of Maj M Y Gran, No 331 (Norwegian)
Sqn, Tangmere, 18 July 1944

**15**
Spitfire IX NH493/FF-J of WO D J Watkins, No 132 Sqn,
B14 Amblie, France, 30 July 1944

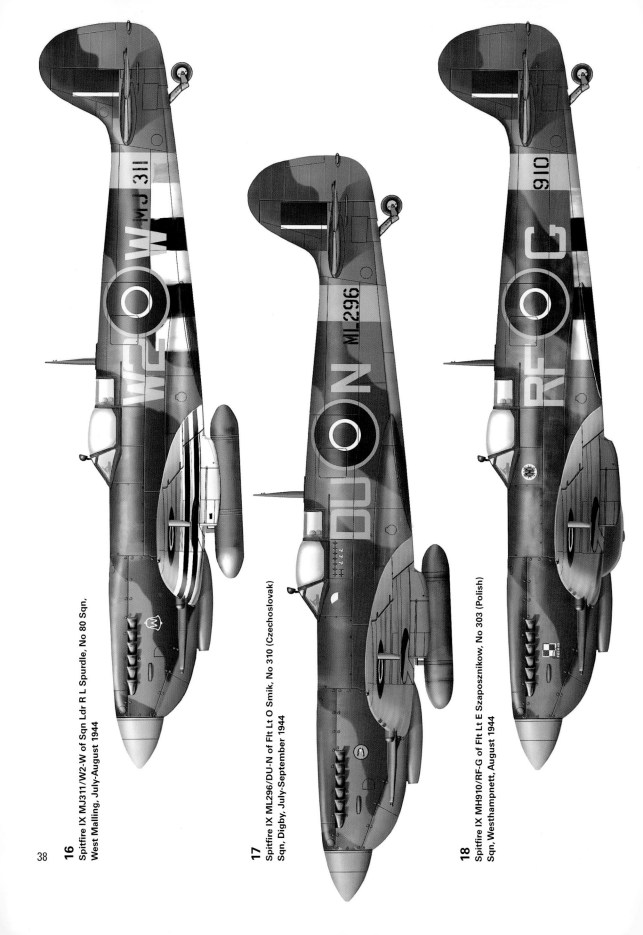

**16**
Spitfire IX MJ311/W2-W of Sqn Ldr R L Spurdle, No 80 Sqn,
West Malling, July-August 1944

**17**
Spitfire IX ML296/DU-N of Flt Lt O Smik, No 310 (Czechoslovak)
Sqn, Digby, July-September 1944

**18**
Spitfire IX MH910/RF-G of Flt Lt E Szaposznikow, No 303 (Polish)
Sqn, Westhampnett, August 1944

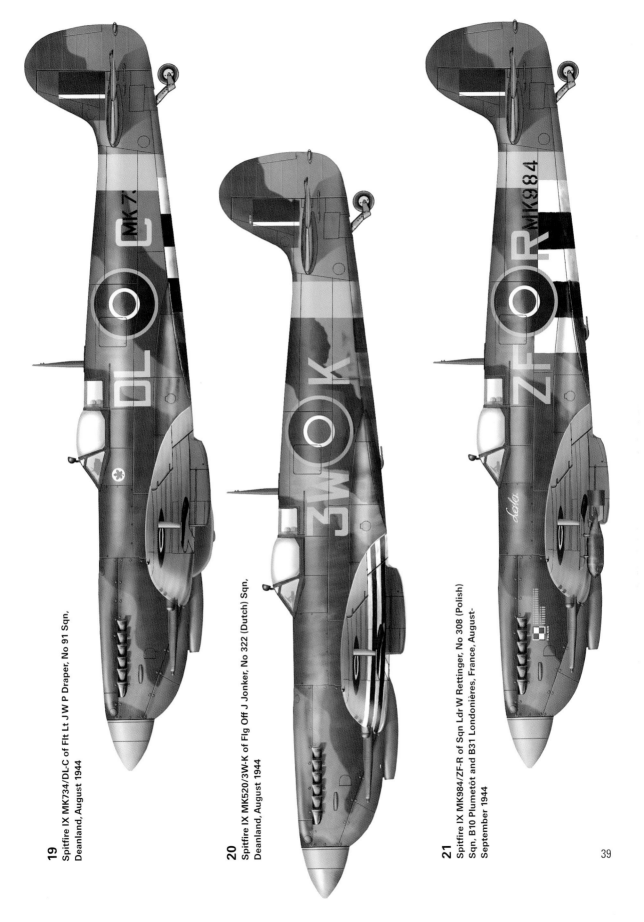

**19**
Spitfire IX MK734/DL-C of Flt Lt J W P Draper, No 91 Sqn,
Deanland, August 1944

**20**
Spitfire IX MK520/3W-K of Flg Off J Jonker, No 322 (Dutch) Sqn,
Deanland, August 1944

**21**
Spitfire IX MK984/ZF-R of Sqn Ldr W Rettinger, No 308 (Polish)
Sqn, B10 Plumetót and B31 Londonières, France, August-
September 1944

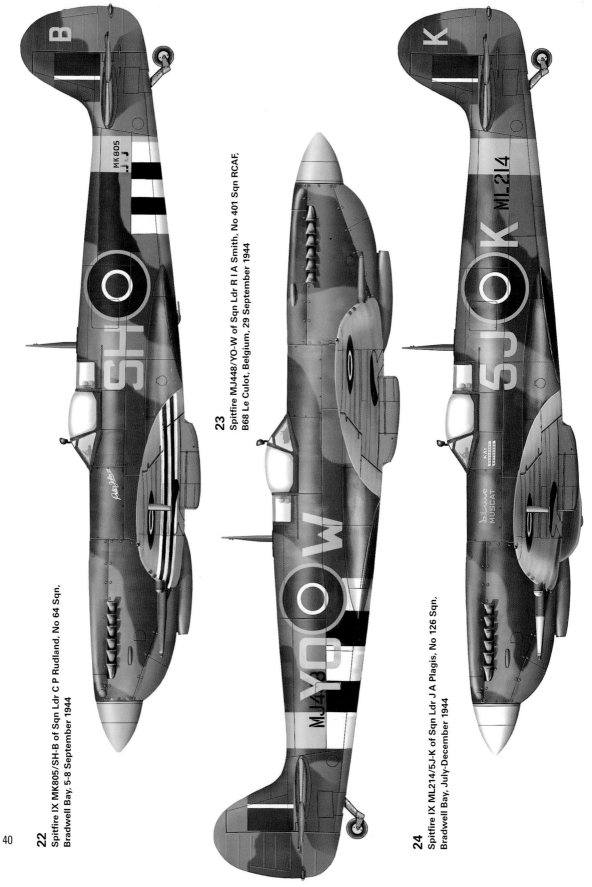

**22**
Spitfire IX MK805/SH-B of Sqn Ldr C P Rudland, No 64 Sqn,
Bradwell Bay, 5-8 September 1944

**23**
Spitfire MJ448/YO-W of Sqn Ldr R I A Smith, No 401 Sqn RCAF,
B68 Le Culot, Belgium, 29 September 1944

**24**
Spitfire IX ML214/5J-K of Sqn Ldr J A Plagis, No 126 Sqn,
Bradwell Bay, July-December 1944

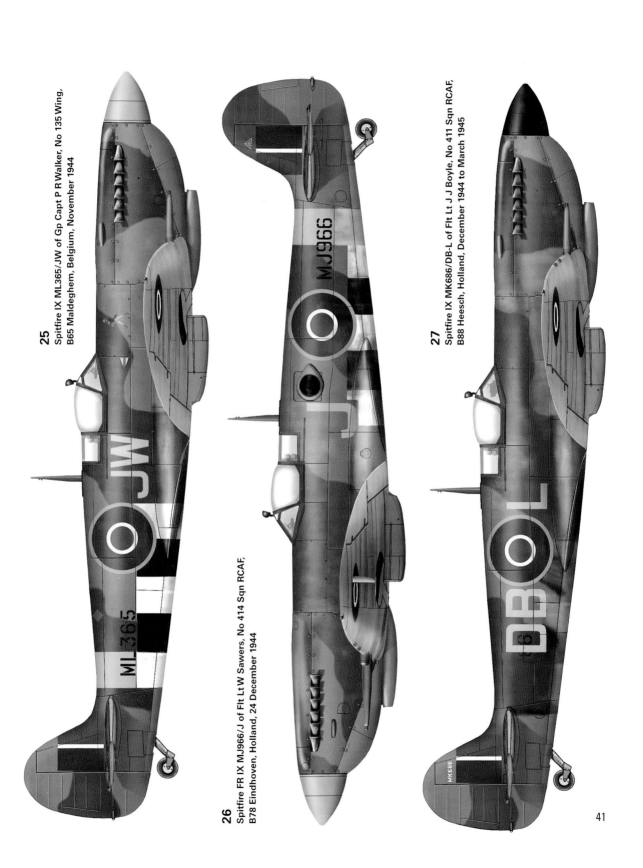

**25**
Spitfire IX ML365/JW of Gp Capt P R Walker, No 135 Wing,
B65 Maldeghem, Belgium, November 1944

**26**
Spitfire FR IX MJ966/J of Flt Lt W Sawers, No 414 Sqn RCAF,
B78 Eindhoven, Holland, 24 December 1944

**27**
Spitfire IX MK686/DB-L of Flt Lt J J Boyle, No 411 Sqn RCAF,
B88 Heesch, Holland, December 1944 to March 1945

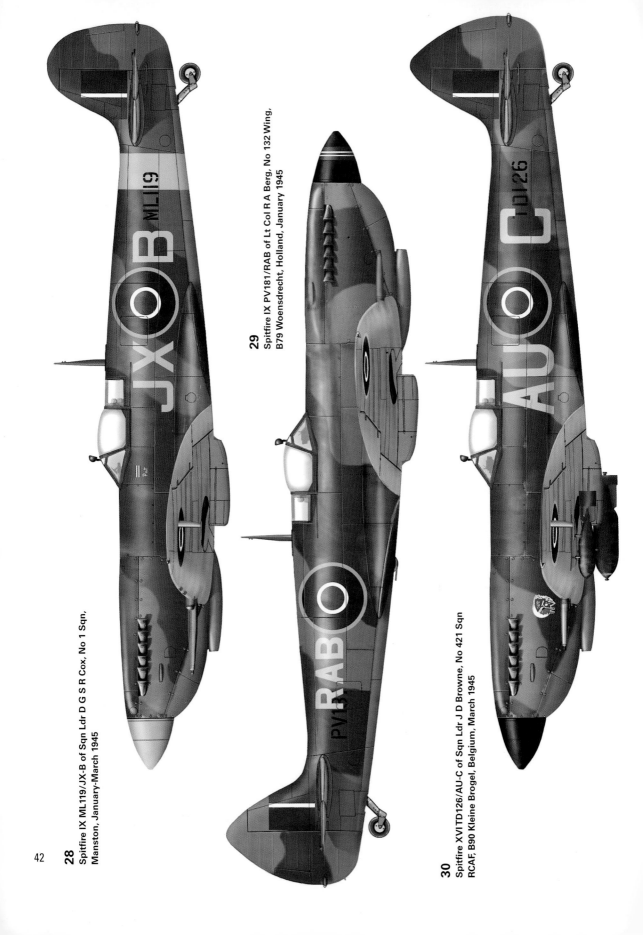

**28**
Spitfire IX ML119/JX-B of Sqn Ldr D G S R Cox, No 1 Sqn, Manston, January-March 1945

**29**
Spitfire IX PV181/RAB of Lt Col R A Berg, No 132 Wing, B79 Woensdrecht, Holland, January 1945

**30**
Spitfire XVI TD126/AU-C of Sqn Ldr J D Browne, No 421 Sqn RCAF, B90 Kleine Brogel, Belgium, March 1945

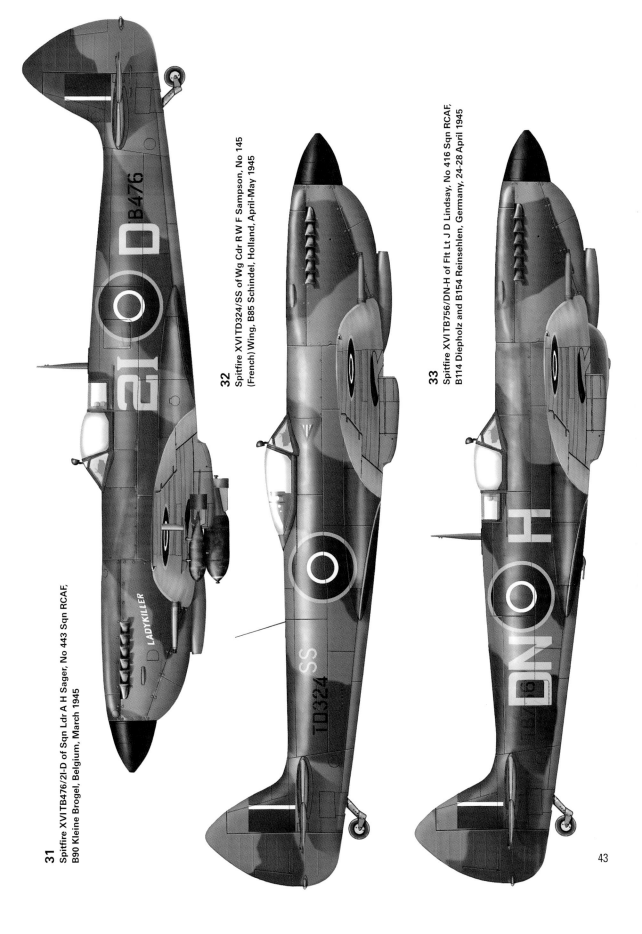

**31**
Spitfire XVI TB476/21-D of Sqn Ldr A H Sager, No 443 Sqn RCAF,
B90 Kleine Brogel, Belgium, March 1945

**32**
Spitfire XVI TD324/SS of Wg Cdr R W F Sampson, No 145
(French) Wing, B85 Schindel, Holland, April-May 1945

**33**
Spitfire XVI TB756/DN-H of Flt Lt J D Lindsay, No 416 Sqn RCAF,
B114 Diepholz and B154 Reinsehlen, Germany, 24-28 April 1945

43

**34**
Spitfire XVI TB900/GE-D of Sqn Ldr R A Lallemant, No 349
(Belgian) Sqn, B106 Twente, Holland, and B113 Varrelbusch,
Germany, April-May 1945

**35**
Spitfire XVI TB752/KH-Z of Sqn Ldr H P M Zary, No 403 Sqn
RCAF, B114 Diepholz, Germany, April-June 1945

**36**
Spitfire XVI TD246/GRM of Gp Capt G R McGregor, No 126 Wing,
B116 Wunstorf and B152 Fassburg, Germany, July-August 1945

Sous-Lt Pierre Clostermann congratulates Flt Lt Ken Charney on becoming an ace after they had each shot down an Fw 190 in combat near Cabourg on the afternoon of 2 July. This was the Frenchman's last victory with the Spitfire (*via Dugald Cameron*)

Sharing Moore's third victory was future ace Flg Off Ron Lake, who also claimed a second Bf 109 and an Fw 190 destroyed.

Then to the east of Caen at 1500 hrs No 403 Sqn had a very successful action that saw its pilots claim eight fighters destroyed. Flt Lt Andy Mackenzie shot down a Bf 109 for his seventh kill, whilst Flt Lt 'Mac' Gordon moved closer to acedom when he was credited with a brace of Messerschmitts. The honours for the day, however, went to James Lindsay, who became an ace in spectacular style by shooting down three Bf 109s. Within an hour another RCAF pilot achieved his fifth success when 22-year-old Flg Off Bill Klersy (in Spitfire IX MK590) of No 401 Sqn got a Bf 109 east of Caen, whilst squadronmate 'Hap' Kennedy achieved his final success in the same action.

Within a few minutes the Spitfires of No 602 Sqn were also in action, having been scrambled to the southeast of Caen. Flt Lt Ken Charney shot down an Fw 190 to also become an ace, and his Free French compatriot Sous-Lt Pierre Clostermann claimed another, as well as four damaged – this proved to be the Frenchman's last Spitfire victory.

During improved weather on 5 July the Luftwaffe's fighters put in a major effort of more than 500 sorties, which in turn resulted in further success for 2nd TAF's Spitfire units, in part due to the effectiveness of the fighter control system that was now well established on the Continent. In the evening the irrepressible 'Johnnie' Johnson led No 441 Sqn into an engagement that saw the unit down eight fighters near Alençon, the Wing Leader claiming two himself. No 441 Sqn's CO, Sqn Ldr Tommy Brannagan got one, as did Flt Lt Guy Mott, who also shared another – both men would later 'make ace'. Finally, opening his account in this action was yet another future ace, Flg Off Don Kimball;

'I attacked the last of the FW 190s, flying in line astern. It broke towards me and I did a steep turn around onto its tail, giving it a short burst with cannon and machine guns. It then rolled and dove. I followed it, and after my second burst it burst into flame and crashed north of Alençon.'

One of the few victories not claimed by the RCAF that day fell to a patrol of No 132 Sqn aircraft that was bounced by around 20 Bf 109s during the afternoon. The enemy fighters came off worse, however, as one was shot down by Flt Lt Mike Graham in Spitfire IX MJ145/FF-A. This victory took him to acedom.

The Norwegians in No 132 Wing remained busy during this period as well, resulting in the creation of more aces. On 6 July, during an escort for Mitchells bombing Chartres, the Allied formation was attacked by 20 German fighters. Wing Leader Lt Col Rolf Berg achieved acedom when he shot down a Bf 109 and an Fw 190, whilst the No 331 Sqn ace Capt Nils Jörstad made his final claims when flying FN-Q, shooting down a brace of Fw 190s to take his tally to seven. His CO, Maj Martin Gran, who was also an ace, shared in the dstruction of a Bf 109, and others shot down two more.

Norwegian pilots of No 331 Sqn debrief at Tangmere after a sortie over the beaches. On the left, smoking a welcome cigarette, is Capt Nils Jörstadt, who became an ace on 20 June. Facing him immediately to his left is a youthful Lt Ragnar Dogger, who was rested soon afterwards but attained ace status later in the year (*Bengt Stangvik*)

6 July also saw a change in the appearance of many aircraft when HQ AEAF ordered some types to carry stripes on the undersurfaces only, and this was followed in August by instructions that all wing stripes should be removed over the next few weeks.

After bitter resistance and almost total destruction of the city of Caen to bombing and artillery fire, it finally fell on 9 July. This allowed British forces to push deeper into Normandy, although they still faced stiff opposition. In the 2nd TAF wings several promotions also occurred, with Geoffrey Page being moved to lead No 125 Wing and his place being taken in No 132 Sqn by Ken Charney. No 442 Sqn's CO, Dal Russel, left to lead No 126 Wing, Sqn Ldr Harry Dowding being promoted in his place. Russel was well respected, and his fellow ace 'Hap' Kennedy said of him, 'Dal was a true gentleman, who the inelegance of war did not change. He was one of the relatively few Canadians in the Battle of Britain, and was on his third tour of operations'.

It was not only the Luftwaffe and the Wehrmacht that fell victim to 2nd TAF's Spitfires, for when flying a beach patrol on 8 July Flt Lt Dean Dover's section from No 442 Sqn spotted five midget submarines near the mouth of the River Orne and, diving down, the four Spitfires sank one of them. Another section led by Flt Lt Wright spotted two more, sinking one of them, and during a further patrol Dover's section destroyed a third. The destruction of these vessels proved to be the exception, however, for German air power remained the main prey.

Indeed, the following afternoon near Lisieux, No 453 Sqn's CO, Sqn Ldr Don Smith, spotted a large number of German fighters above him and casually radioed to his unit, 'Look above you and you'll see something interesting'. He then began a power climb, leading a head-on attack on the enemy formation. In the brief fight that ensued Smith shot down a Bf 109 for his final victory, and two more were destroyed by the squadron in an action in which not a single Spitfire was hit.

The Canadians continued their successes when, west of Argentan on the 13th, Sqn Ldr Tommy Brannagan of No 441 Sqn hit two Fw 190s that exploded. Flt Lt Guy Mott witnessed his CO become an ace, before claiming a fighter himself;

Sqn Ldr Don Smith (standing) and some of his pilots relax outside a French café after moving to France, where he claimed his sixth, and final, victory on 9 July (*RAAF*)

'I saw two blow up and then started chasing two FW 190s on the deck. I saw strikes on one of the FW 190s at two different times, after which the pilot jettisoned his canopy, pulled up to around 500 ft and bailed out.'

Another Focke-Wulf fell to Flg Off Don Kimball, while Flt Lt William Myers downed no fewer than three Fw 190s – his only successes. This feat earned him a DFC. In all, No 441 Sqn claimed ten German fighters destroyed. The following day (14 July – Bastille Day) Sqn Ldr Ken Charney of No 132 Sqn, in company with his predecessor Wg Cdr Geoffrey Page, flew what was ostensibly a cannon test flight. However, as they neared Argentan they bounced three Fw 190s and destroyed one apiece. Charney wrote of his final victory;

'I attacked a FW 190 in a climbing turn near the base of a cloud. I saw strikes around his tail unit and fuselage on the starboard side just as the enemy aircraft pulled into the cloud. He reappeared immediately, inverted, and started spinning at 2000 ft. I watched him go straight into the ground, where he blew up.'

An hour earlier, No 416 Sqn had had its most successful aerial engagement of the war to date when Spitfire IXs led by Flt Lt Danny Noonan scrambled over Pont L'Eveque to support a patrol. Noonan became an ace during the course of the action, as he described in his combat report;

'I engaged a Me 109 at about 600 yards, closing to 300 yards. There were cannon and machine gun strikes around the cockpit and fuselage, and after giving four short bursts I saw a flash and then broke to port onto the tail of another Me 109. The pilot of the first Me 109 was seen to bail out.'

Noonan then went after the second Messerschmitt, which he crippled before calling in Flg Off Bud Fraser to finish it off. In all, No 416 Sqn destroyed seven German fighters during the course of the day.

As the battles on the ground continued to their bloody conclusion, the fighting in the air over Normandy remained intense. Among those involved in the action was No 602 Sqn's high-scoring CO, South African Sqn Ldr Chris Le Roux, who claimed two Fw 190s and a Bf 109 on 15-16 July. However, it is likely that his greatest contribution to Allied success in Normandy may have come on the afternoon of 17 July when he led an armed reconnaissance over enemy territory. At about 1615 hrs he shot down a Bf 109 near Flers and, more significantly, he then strafed a staff car that was later assessed to have been carrying Generalfeldmarschall Erwin Rommel. The commander of Army Group B was gravely wounded. Le Roux's day was not yet over, for that evening he shot down his fifth fighter in as many days.

Several hours earlier, Spitfire IXs of No 412 Sqn, led by Flt Lt Charley Fox, were also out on an armed reconnaissance in the same area as No 602 Sqn. Fox dived on a large Horch convertible staff car carrying four officers and a driver and opened fire, causing it to crash into a ditch. He submitted his report, and when news of the loss of the legendary 'Desert Fox' was subsequently received No 126 Wing's Intelligence officer suggested that Fox had been responsible, and thus entered this significant 'scalp' in his logbook.

Mid July also saw some significant reorganisation of the 2nd TAF Spitfire wings, resulting in the break up of No 144 Wing and the sharing of its units amongst other wings. No 441 Sqn went to No 125 Wing, No 442 Sqn to No 126 Wing and No 443 Sqn to No 127 Wing, the latter also gaining 'Johnnie' Johnson as its leader in place of seven-victory ace Wg Cdr Bob Buckham, who was tour expired. Some wing COs changed too, with aces Gp Capts Jamie Rankin and Gordon McGregor taking over Nos 125 and 126 Wings, respectively. Wg Cdr Ray Harries, a highly successful ace, also arrived as the No 135 Wing Wing Leader, and he was soon back in the swing by claiming his 18th, and last, victory on 25 July when he shot down an Fw 190 near Routat. Harries and No 485 Sqn's CO, Sqn Ldr John Niven, were old friends who used to entertain the pilots with their piano-playing duos!

Dawn on 18 July saw a massive attack by more than 4000 RAF and USAAF bombers to mark the start of Operation *Goodwood* – the breakout assault of the British 2nd Army, which despite heavy tank losses made steady progress. The only victories during the day fell to No 441 Sqn, which ran into a pair of Bf 109s, both of which were shot down. One fell to Flt Lt Guy Mott to take him to acedom. Losses to ground fire were heavy, however, and included No 421 Sqn ace Flt Lt Paul Johnson.

Flt Lt Wilfred Banks of No 421 Sqn attained ace status in spectacular fashion when, on the afternoon of the 24th southeast of Lisieux, he shot down two Bf 109s and an Fw 190 to take his score to six. Squadronmate Plt Off David Jamieson bagged two Bf 109s to also become an ace shortly thereafter. That same day No 412 Sqn's Flt Lt 'Ossie' Linton got two Focke-Wulfs to take his score to 3.5, but frustratingly he did not manage to get his fifth kill before returning to Canada. ADGB units were also involved in the action on 24 July

After becoming CO of No 602 Sqn in July 1944, Sqn Ldr Chris Le Roux claimed six victories to take his total to 18 before his death in a flying accident in late August. He is probably best remembered for leading the strafing attack on a staff car on 17 July 1944 that severely wounded Generalfeldmarschall Erwin Rommel (*via Dugald Cameron*)

On 24 July Flt Lt Wilf Banks of No 412 Sqn shot down three Bf 109s to become an ace, and in the process claimed No 126 Wing's 100th victory and so won the sweepstake! (*PAC*)

Sqn Ldr Johnny Plagis was the most successful Rhodesian pilot of World War 2. In July 1944 he took command of No 126 Sqn, and within weeks he had claimed three victories to take his total to 17. He usually flew Spitfire IX ML214/5J-K, a presentation aircraft christened *Muscat* that he named after his sister and added his scoreboard to (*Mrs Beryl Salt*)

when ace Sqn Ldr Johnnie Plagis (the newly arrived CO of No 126 Sqn, flying Spitfire IX ML214/5J-K) brought down a Bf 109 near Angers for his first victory of the tour. A second Messerschmitt was credited to Flt Lt Ron Collis during the same engagement.

After delays due to heavy rain, further carpet-bombing by USAAF 'heavies' on 25 July was followed by another tank assault and plenty of action for 2nd TAF units ranging far behind enemy lines on armed reconnaissance, as No 453 Sqn's CO Sqn Ldr Don Smith described to a reporter;

'Three aircraft on an armed reconnaissance spotted nine large German fuel tankers moving along a road. Seven of them went up in flames very smartly. Later, a tank commander sent a message of congratulation.'

The outstanding performance of the day, however, came from Flt Lt Henry Zary of No 421 Sqn, who managed a hat trick of Bf 109 victories over Les Andelys. Having shot down two in short order, Zary then had to chase the third fighter as it hedgehopped across the French countryside. 'I fired at the last enemy aircraft, which dived to the deck and I followed. I was out of ammunition, but remained above and behind him. I then dived on the enemy anyhow. The enemy aircraft turned sharply to starboard to evade and then apparently hit a tree, for it stalled into the ground', Zary explained in his combat report.

Despite being battered on the ground and in the air, German forces grimly defended Normandy into August. On the 1st the Harrowbeer Wing Leader, Wg Cdr Harold 'Birdy' Bird-Wilson, was leading a sweep over Angers airfield when, flying Spitfire IX ML397/5J-D of No 126 Sqn, he shot down a Bf 109G to claim his final victory. Minutes later he strafed and destroyed a Do 217 on the ground. Also successful during the day was Wg Cdr Johnny Checketts, who, on a sweep near Livarot, shot down a Bf 109 for his penultimate victory. However, during an armed reconnaissance by No 412 Sqn the following afternoon Sqn Ldr Jack Sheppard became embroiled with some Bf 109s near Argentan and was shot down by Unteroffizier Anton Schoeppler of I./JG 5. He evaded capture and returned to Allied lines ten days later – Sqn Ldr Dean Dover took over the unit. During the afternoon of 3 August Flt Lt James Lindsay ended his tour with No 403 Sqn in some style;

'I spotted 20+ Me 109s flying due east over Laigle, 4000 ft below. I broke around and gave chase, closing very slowly. I noticed another aircraft straggling on my right and broke around onto him. I opened fire, closing to 50 yards. I saw strikes on the wing roots and tail. The enemy aircraft poured white smoke and pieces fell off, including the tail, I saw the enemy aircraft crash into a field northwest of Dreux.'

Lindsay saw further combat when he returned to No 403 Sqn just before the war ended, and he also enjoyed aerial success flying F-86s over Korea.

49

Following several quiet days in the air, on the afternoon of 8 August desert ace Flt Lt 'Gordie' Troke of No 443 Sqn shot down a Bf 109 for his first, slightly unusual, success in Normandy. 'I led the section in a turn to starboard and positioned myself above and behind the enemy aircraft', Troke noted in his combat report. 'When at a range of 1000 yards from him, the enemy pilot rolled onto his back and bailed out. The enemy aircraft was seen to crash'.

British-based ADGB squadrons also remained active over the wider battlefront during this period. On 7 August, for example, Spitfire VIIs of No 131 Sqn flew a 'Rodeo' along the valley of the River Loire. It was led by Wg Cdr Pete Brothers, who invited Sqn Ldr Sammy Sampson from HQ No 10 Group to participate. Near Chateau Blois they spotted some Fw 190s, and in the ensuing fight Brothers' 'guest' shot one down;

'The Spitfire VII can easily out-turn a '190, and easier still if the '190 pilot opens his throttle. He started to climb off the deck and began to weave about. When I was about 250 yards away I gave him two more bursts of three seconds each, and the Focke-Wulf went over straight into the ground and exploded.'

Pete Brothers got a second fighter for his 16th, and last, victory;

'As I closed the range I was surprised to see my '190 start a gentle climb, weaving equally gently to the left and the right, offering a perfect target. "Oh, my God, you poor sucker. You must be straight out of training school", I thought. It seemed so unfair, and spoilt the exhilaration of the chase. This was not to be an exciting duel, but a massacre. Worse was to follow. I opened fire and was horrified and sickened to see my cannon

Once on the Continent, most maintenance was done in the open. Here, Spitfire IX MK304/Y2-K of No 442 Sqn has its engine changed on 19 August. Flying the fighter on the afternoon of 30 June, Flt Lt Dean Dover had shot down an Fw 190 to claim his third victory. Earlier in the day Flt Lt Arnold Roseland had also shot down a Focke-Wulf fighter and shared in the destruction of a second (*DND*)

No 441 Sqn's CO, Sqn Ldr Tommy Brannagan, relaxes under a tree adjacent to Spitfire IX NH320/9G-W in which, on 13 July, he had shot down two Fw 190s to become an ace. He fell victim to flak on 15 August and became a PoW (*via C H Thomas*)

shells not knock off a wing or tail of the aircraft, but blast straight into the cockpit, instantly killing the pilot. The aircraft flipped over and hit the ground. "I am sorry, I didn't mean that", I said out loud.'

For most of the ADGB squadrons, bomber escorts predominated, such as when 24 aircraft from Detling-based Nos 1 and 165 Sqns, led by nine-victory ace Wg Cdr Peter Powell, gave close escort to 36 A-20 Bostons attacking a rail junction. Sadly, during a sweep over Belgium on the 15th No 91 Sqn's CO, Sqn Ldr Norman Kynaston, was hit by flak and lost. It was not a good day for aces as during an evening armed reconnaissance No 441 Sqn's CO, Sqn Ldr Tommy Brannagan, was hit by flak near Bernay and forced to crash land. He soon became a PoW.

Meanwhile, the ground campaign reached its climax, with the Canadians thrusting towards the Seine. When they took Falaise on 17 August there remained just a gap of five miles in the Allied pincer through which the defeated 7th *Armee* desperately tried to escape. With Allied fighter-bombers reigning supreme, it was a corridor of death, as the daily report of the 5th *PanzerArmee* stated – 'Any movement or assembly of units impossible'. The Spitfire units took a grim toll in their strafing attacks, albeit at a cost of steady losses. Typical of the pilots involved in these missions was No 411 Sqn's new CO, Sqn Ldr Bob Hayward, who flew four ground attack sorties on 17 August. He noted in his logbook '24 enemy vehicles destroyed – "flamers"; four badly shot up – "smokers"; and ten damaged'. He also noted that this was 'a very economical way to beat the Germans!'

On 19 August Generalfeldmarschall Walther Model, the commander-in-chief of Army Group B and OB West, ordered 7th *Armee* to withdraw, but by then it was too late and his forces were in chaos. In the face of mounting losses from relentless attacks, the Wehrmacht struggled to keep open the gap to enable their withdrawal across the Seine. It was the day Gen Bernard Montgomery considered the difficult two-month long Battle for Normandy over.

# ON TO THE RHINE

By 22 August 7th *Armee* had to all intents been destroyed, having abandoned most of its heavy equipment. The scene was now set for a rapid Allied advance into France. Attacks on surviving German forces struggling to cross the Seine continued, and it was estimated that around 40 Wehrmacht divisions were destroyed during the battle for Normandy. As the Allied armies pursued their defeated enemy, so the fighter sweeps spread ahead, encountering the Luftwaffe as it attempted to provide such cover as it could in the face of massive Allied air superiority.

On the 23rd, for example, 'Johnnie' Johnson led Nos 421 and 443 Sqns on a sweep of the Paris area. Near Senlis the Spitfire pilots engaged a large force of Fw 190s and Bf 109s. Keeping No 421 Sqn as top cover, he led No 443 Sqn in an interception of the enemy fighters. Six of the latter were shot down, including two by Johnson himself. Above them, No 421 Sqn claimed six more, including one to Flt Lt John Neil to make him an ace. Minutes later he was in turn forced to bail out and was captured. Despite his success, Johnson was impressed by the performance of his opponents during the fight. 'I was attacked by six short-nosed '190s, which possessed an exceptional rate of climb. By turning into each attack I managed to evade most of their fire, only receiving one hit in the starboard wing root'. Nevertheless, it had been a perfect bounce.

With more landing grounds now available further 2nd TAF Spitfire units moved into Normandy, including the Free French No 145 Wing which made an emotional move into B8 Sommerviue. It was followed shortly thereafter by the Norwegian No 132 Wing, which was based at B16 Villons les Buissons, and No 135 Wing at B17 Carpiquet. For many Wings the move across the Channel was the start of an itinerant existence as they attempted to keep up with the advancing frontline. For example, on 21 August No 127 Sqn moved to the Continent, where it flew fighter-bomber missions from various airfields in France, Belgium and Holland through to VE Day. It achieved a rare success for a dedicated fighter-bomber squadron when, south of Boos, on 25 August (the day Paris was liberated) the unit had had a fight with a trio of Fw 190s, one of which was shot down by the CO, Sqn Ldr Frank Bradley, in Spitfire IX NH583.

The following morning 12 Spitfires from No 416 Sqn were on patrol east of Rouen when they spotted German fighters above them. Climbing up to engage the aircraft, Flt Lt Dave Harling attacked a straggler. As it broke away, the 23-year-old followed the Fw 190 down, firing short bursts until it hit the ground. Harling had claimed the first of his five victories. In the same area soon afterwards, Sqn Ldr Don Smith and his Australian pilots from No 453 Sqn intercepted 20+ Bf 109s. In the sharp fight that ensued three were probably destroyed, with Smith's claim being his last.

ADGB Spitfires increasingly provided escorts for daylight raids by Bomber Command 'heavies', the latter mainly attacking targets in the Ruhr. Here, flak proved the main threat, which was an indication of how the situation in the air was changing. On 27 August Bomber Command mounted its first major daylight raid on Germany since 1941 with an

After No 91 Sqn re-equipped with Spitfire IXs in August 1944, its first operation with the new type was to provide the escort for a Lancaster raid on Douai. MK734/DL-C participated in the mission, with five-victory ace Flt Lt John Draper at the controls. It was subsequently flown by a number of notable pilots through the autumn, including Wg Cdr Bobby Oxspring, and on 5 December Flg Off Faulkner used MK734 to shoot down a Bf 109 (*E B Morgan*)

attack against a synthetic oil refinery near Homberg, on the Ruhr. The heavy escort included Spitfire IXs from No 1 Sqn, led by Malta ace Sqn Ldr Pat Lardner-Burke, that were fitted with the unwieldy and unpopular 90-gallon overload tanks for the 2.5-hour mission.

The day also saw the loss of a significant fighter pilot when, in the early evening whilst leading No 317 Sqn on a sweep over the Seine, Sqn Ldr Wladek Gnys was hit and force landed. Wounded in the chest, he eventually escaped back to Allied lines. Over his native Poland on 1 September 1939, he had shot down two Do 17s to claim the very first victories against the Luftwaffe in World War 2. Gnys was but one of a growing number of Spitfire pilots who had fallen victim to ground fire as the hammering of retreating German forces continued unabated.

The Dutch-manned No 322 Sqn was hit particularly hard. On 1 September Maj Keith Kuhlmann (its seconded SAAF CO, who had nine claims, including four destroyed, to his name) was hit by flak on an armed reconnaissance and had to bail out inland from Cap Gris Nez. He was soon captured. On the same sortie both flight commanders, each of them V1 aces, were also lost. Flt Lt Jan Plesman had his tail shot off by flak near St Omer and crashed to his death, whilst Flt Lt L C M van Eendenburg was more fortunate as he crash-landed southeast of Lille and evaded capture. It had been a tough day for the Dutch unit.

However, such was the speed of the German withdrawal that targets were soon beyond the limited range of the Spitfire units, necessitating frequent changes of base that in turn adversely affected the sortie rate. As September began Rouen and Dieppe were captured, but bad weather constrained aerial operations. The armoured spearheads continued to drive north into Belgium, nevertheless, with Brussels being liberated on the 3rd and the vital port at Antwerp a day later. 2nd TAF wings continued to leapfrog to maintain contact and support, despite the constrictions of the weather. For example, on the 6th Sqn Ldr Hugh Trainor's No 401 Sqn led No 126 Wing into B56 at Brussels/Evere – it was the first RAF fighter unit to be based on Belgian soil.

2nd TAF also began to split its forces at this point, with No 83 Group units supporting the push northeast by the 2nd Army, whilst No 84 Group covered the Canadian 1st Army as it moved up the coastal belt. It was the former that was thus to encounter the Luftwaffe more regularly in the coming weeks. The headlong pace of the advance also slowed as the logistics tail caught up, and planning for the drive into Holland continued. The latter offensive would culminate in the disaster at Arnhem.

## ARNHEM REVERSE

There had been a marked reduction in aerial combat in recent weeks that in some ways led to a false sense of security creeping in to Allied ranks. Several large airborne operations had been planned, and cancelled, but finally Operation *Market Garden* was approved. This envisaged the seizure by airborne forces of vital bridges in Holland at Eindhoven, Nijmegen and Arnhem ahead of an armoured thrust by XXX Corps north from Belgium to outflank the defences of the 'Siegfried Line'. The furthest target was the bridge at Arnhem, and the operation was to result in the resumption of savage aerial fighting. On the eve of *Market Garden* the disposition of 2nd TAF Spitfire units was as follows;

**No 83 Group**

| | |
|---|---|
| No 125 Wing at B52 Douai* | Nos 132, 441, 453 and 602 Sqns |
| No 126 (RCAF) Wing at B56 Evere | Nos 401, 411, 412 and 442 Sqns |
| No 127 (RCAF) Wing at B26 Illiers l'Eveque | Nos 403, 416, 421 and 443 Sqns |

**No 84 Group**

| | |
|---|---|
| No 131 (Polish) Wing at B31 Fresnoy | Nos 302, 308 and 317 Sqns |
| No 132 (Norwegian) Wing at B57 Lille Nord | Nos 66, 127, 331 and 332 Sqns |
| No 135 Wing at B53 Merville | Nos 33, 222, 349 and 485 Sqns |
| No 145 (French) Wing at B51 Lille Vendeville* | Nos 74, 329, 340 and 341 Sqns |

* both were to move the next day

In addition, in Britain the weight of the ADGB day fighter units stood by to escort the vast aerial trains of vulnerable transports and gliders that were to carry the men of the 1st Allied Airborne Army into battle. It was these units that would initially cover the drop, and they included;

Nos 1 and 165 Sqns at Detling
Nos 64, 126 and 611 Sqns at Bradwell Bay
Nos 91 and 345 Sqns at Deanland
Nos 118, 124 and 303 Sqns at Westhampnett
No 131 Sqn at Friston
Nos 229 and 316 Sqns at Coltishall
Nos 234, 310 and 312 Sqns at North Weald
No 504 Sqn at Manston

When French-manned No 345 Sqn received Spitfire IXs in September 1944, its CO, Cdt Jean-Marie Accart, adopted PT766/2Y-A as his own mount. He flew it throughout that month, including during hazardous escort missions for transport aircraft flying in supplies during the ill-fated Arnhem operation (*Gen J-M Accart*)

The beginning of September had also witnessed the new horror of the V2 rocket unleashed on London, and many fighter patrols were mounted over Holland to try to neutralise their mobile launch sites. Operation *Big Ben* missions occupied many East Anglia-based Spitfire units through to war's end.

On the afternoon of 17 September the massive air armada assembled over England and flew under heavy escort across Belgium to the drop zones in Holland, with 2nd TAF and USAAF Ninth Air Force fighters conducting flak suppression ahead of the transports. *Market Garden* provoked a furious enemy response both on the ground and in the air, as it was immediately evident of the threat the operation posed to Germany itself. Near Emmerich around 50 fighters were spotted, but they were held at bay.

Many ADGB Spitfire squadrons escorted the huge formations, with Pat Lardner-Burke of No 1 Sqn noting that *Market Garden* was clearly a big deal for the operation order that came out of the teleprinter was 12 ft long! Another who witnessed the event was ace Wg Cdr Bobby Oxspring;

'Weaving over the train of C-47 tugs, we escorted the first wave of glider-borne troops to the drop zone at Arnhem. It was a spectacular sight as the Horsa gliders rammed the deck from all angles, some breaking up in collisions with trees or other obstacles. We had to admire these airborne boys – what a way to get pitched into combat.'

The Eindhoven bridges were soon captured, and the following day the RCAF Spitfire units were involved when defending the Nijmegen area as the second drop was inbound. No 401 Sqn's Flg Off Robert Davenport shot down an Fw 190 near Venlo to claim his fourth success, and within a few minutes a patrol from No 441 Sqn had destroyed two Bf 109s. Three hours later over Aachen Flt Lt Ron Lake shot down another Messerschmitt for his fourth victory – he would become an ace before the month was out.

Although there were significant transport losses during the landings, none fell to fighters. However, the weather remained unsettled, interfering with air operations. The third lift into what was already becoming a difficult situation on the ground went in on 19 September, following which there were daily re-supply missions. The position of the British 1st Airborne Division at Arnhem was becoming increasingly untenable following the slowing of the XXX Corps advance by a determined enemy, who had been expected to retreat in the face of Allied armour and air power. This meant that the Waal Bridge at Nijmegen was not secured until the 20th. The next day there were further re-supply missions into Arnhem, but for the first time the transports were intercepted by the Luftwaffe. No fewer than 16 Dakotas and 14 Stirlings fell to flak and fighters, Wg Cdr Bobby Oxspring witnessing the carnage;

'We in No 141 Wing, based at Manston, duly rendezvoused with our Dakota charges at Eindhoven and watched them stream into the German flak around Arnhem, some 40 miles away. Flickers of sunlight winked from what we mistakenly took to be the Thunderbolt cover. Suddenly, a couple of "Daks" exploded in fireballs, and the stark truth struck us as we eyeballed a number of fighters peeling out of attacks. We poured on the coals and roared in on more than a dozen FW 190s as they started to wreak carnage among the defenceless "Daks". Before we could engage them, the Focke-Wulfs refused a fight and took off eastwards at high speed. We hung around until the last Dakotas completed their drops and dutifully covered their withdrawal. Our admiration was absolute.'

The only claim by a 2nd TAF Spitfire on 21 September was made by Flt Lt 'Sammy' Hall of No 414 Sqn, who began his path to becoming one of the very few fighter-reconnaissance aces when he shot down an Fw 190 southwest of Nijmegen.

With Arnhem now largely sealed off, the Germans made determined efforts to destroy the bridge at Nijmegen. During one patrol on the afternoon of 25 September, No 441 Sqn engaged 30 Bf 109s trying to bomb the bridge. In the ensuing fight the unit claimed three victories, two falling to Flg Off Don Kimball (in ML141/9G-H) that took him to acedom. When No 401 Sqn also became embroiled in the fight Flt Lt George Johnson claimed two more to take his total to eight, whilst Flt Lt Russ Bouskill increased his score to four – he reached ace status a few days later.

Twenty minutes later No 421 Sqn arrived on the scene, claiming three victories. Two of these fell to the guns of Flt Lt John Mitchner, who had become an ace with No 402 Sqn during 1943 and then returned for a further tour. At 1530 hrs, in mist and rain and with cumulus towering above 16,000 ft, Flt Lt Art Sager led a patrol from No 416 Sqn as high cover over the Arnhem area in company with No 412 Sqn. A formation of Fw 190s was soon engaged and three German fighters were destroyed, including one claimed by No 416 Sqn's Flt Lt Neil Russell and another credited to No 421 Sqn's Flt Lt Don Laubman for his seventh success. No 421 Sqn lost two Spitfires in the clash, however.

Spitfires based in southeast England also conducted patrols over Arnhem on 25 September, with No 118 Sqn's Flt Lt Ken Giddings destroying a Bf 109 over the town in concert with No 142 Wing Leader

Wg Cdr Johnny Checketts was one of New Zealand's most successful aces in World War 2, and while leading No 142 Wing he claimed his last victory, over Arnhem, on 25 September when he shared in the destruction of a Bf 109 (*RNZAF*)

On 25 September Johnny Checketts was flying his personally marked Spitfire IX ML350/JMC (*via C H Thomas*)

Wg Cdr Johnny Checketts (who was flying Spitfire IX ML350/JMC). This was the New Zealander's 14th, and last, victory, and the share also made Giddings an ace.

Although Arnhem was lost on 26 September, the aerial fighting overhead remained intense. Indeed, on that day Spitfires were credited with 14 aircraft destroyed. The first fell to No 416 Sqn, closely followed by a Bf 109 to No 132 Sqn ace Flt Lt Mike Graham at 1315 hrs – this was his final victory. Not to be outdone, No 125 Wing Wing Leader Wg Cdr Geoffrey Page shot down another Bf 109 for his last success several hours later. Hitting the fighter in a dive that had started at 10,000 ft, he had 'half-rolled onto him and opened fire from 400 yards, closing to 150 yards dead astern. I fired two short bursts, and with the second burst I saw strikes on the starboard wing. Black smoke poured from the enemy aircraft. I overshot it and went out to one side. The enemy aircraft dived steeply through cloud and Flg Off Darraugh saw it crash'.

The day, however, belonged to No 412 Sqn, which in two combats despatched ten fighters. Just to the east of Nijmegen Flt Lt Rod Smith got a pair of Bf 109s, whilst fellow aces Flt Lts Don Laubman and Wilfred Banks each shot down two Fw 190s, with Flg Off Philip Charron getting one for his fourth victory. He did not have to wait long to get his fifth, for three hours later, in the same area, he shot down another Bf 109, as did Don Laubman.

Ominously, however, that evening ace Flg Off Frank Campbell of No 132 Sqn (in Spitfire IX PL257/FF-T) encountered an Me 262 jet that he chased and managed to damage before it flew off at high speed. His final claim was also 2nd TAF's first against this revolutionary aircraft.

27 September was another day of heavy action over the Dutch/German border area as fighting continued around the approaches to Arnhem. The Luftwaffe redoubled its efforts to drop the Rhine bridges, and this resulted in intense fighting that saw the defenders submit claims for no fewer than 45 victories – all but six by RCAF Spitfire units. First up was No 441 Sqn, which bagged three Bf 109s over Arnhem. Amongst the successful pilots was Flt Lt Ron Lake, who 'made ace' with this kill. No 412 Sqn was next

in action when, during a lunchtime patrol, Flt Lt Charlie Fox took his tally to four destroyed in a fight between Arnhem and Nijmegen shortly before 1300 hrs. He shot down two Fw 190s, whilst the Bf 109 claimed by Flg Off Lloyd Berryman was his fourth success as well. Frustratingly, neither pilot would score that all-important fifth victory.

In what was a good day for No 412 Sqn, during a later patrol four more German fighters were shot down. One of these gave Don Laubman his fourth success for the 27th, while Flt Lt David Jamieson shot down two Fw 190s for his final claims.

At around midday Wg Cdr 'Johnnie' Johnson (again in Spitfire IX MK392/JEJ) led No 443 Sqn on patrol over the town of Rees, as he described in his combat report;

'I saw nine ME 109s flying at ground level immediately below us. I led the squadron down to attack but enemy aircraft saw us and broke upwards into the attack, and a general melee ensued. I closed to 250 yards on a ME 109 turning to port, firing short bursts of cannon and machine gun. Strikes were seen on the port wing of the enemy aircraft. He peeled away and crashed into the ground.'

This was Johnson's final success, taking his tally to 34 and seven shared victories. No 443 Sqn's pilots claimed four more. However, this success came at a heavy cost, for Sqn Ldr Wally McLeod chased after the enemy leader and was not seen again. His body was later found in the wreckage of his Spitfire, McLeod having possibly been shot down by Major Siegfried Freytag, *Kommodore* of JG 77, the Canadian being his 101st kill. With 21 victories to his name, the 29-year-old McLeod was the top scoring RCAF pilot of the war.

Earlier, No 411 Sqn's Flt Lt Esli Lapp had shot down two Fw 190s and, just after lunch, he and Flg Off Bob Cook found a solitary Me 410 over Nijmegen and shot it down, the share taking Lapp to acedom. Also reaching this milestone was Flt Lt Art Sager, who had encountered 50 enemy fighters

Operation *Market Garden* resulted in much heavy aerial fighting, and Canadian Flt Lt Elgin 'Irish' Ireland of No 411 Sqn found himself in the thick of the action on 27 September. Although his aircraft, MJ536/DB-W, was badly damaged by cannon rounds fired by an Fw 190, he swiftly exacted his revenge by shooting down another Focke-Wulf during the same action. By VE Day Ireland had claimed three aircraft shot down and one damaged (the latter was an Me 262) (*E G Ireland*) over Nijmegen while leading No 416 Sqn. Employing breaking cloud to mask their approach, the smaller formation of RCAF Spitfires used the element of surprise to overwhelm their more numerous enemy. Flt Lt Dave Harling sent down an Fw 190 with a single burst, and as a Bf 109 tried to get at him he broke around it and put several bursts of accurate fire into the fighter's wings and fuselage, causing it to crash-land at high speed and cart wheel to destruction. Art Sager also shot down a Focke-Wulf in flames to achieve his fifth confirmed victory. Continuing east, he encountered a group of Bf 109s near Emmerich, which he attacked despite being hit by flak. Sager saw an explosion in the cockpit before blowing the fighter's tail off. These were the final victories in what had been an extraordinary day.

## First Jet Victory

German jets were now being seen regularly over Holland, and on 28 September Flt Lt James 'Chips' McColl of No 416 Sqn damaged an Me 262 near Nijmegen. Despite deteriorating weather, the Nijmegen area continued to be a focus for Luftwaffe activity, resulting in another upsurge in aerial fighting. Indeed, on 29 September 35 enemy fighters were claimed, the majority by Canadian Spitfire pilots, resulting in five more aces being created.

On one of his first patrols since taking command, Sqn Ldr Rod Smith (flying MJ448/YO-W) led No 401 Sqn on a mid-morning flight that saw the unit engage more than 30 enemy fighters. Smith claimed two Bf 109s, as did Flt Lt Hedley Everard and Flg Offs Doug Husband and John Hughes, whilst Flt Lt Russ Bouskill claimed a single success. These victories took Smith's tally to 11, while the remaining quartet of pilots 'made ace' with their successes. 'Snooks' Everard, whose earlier victories had been achieved over Burma and Italy, recalled how he claimed the second of his two kills;

'The second dogfight began immediately after the first one had finished, the victim being the aircraft nearest to me in the remainder of the formation, which still milled about on the deck. I gave this aircraft two two-second bursts from 70 yards quarter astern. On the second

**Flying Spitfire IX MJ448/YO-W on 29 September, No 401 Sqn CO Sqn Ldr Rod Smith shot down two Bf 109s that proved to be his penultimate successes (*via C H Thomas*)**

burst it exploded, and I was unable to steer clear of the debris. Part of the pilot's body hit my mainplane inboard of the starboard cannon and dented it.'

Within minutes No 421 Sqn also joined in the action and claimed another five German fighters.

Flying with No 443 Sqn a few hours later, Flg Off Gordon Ockenden destroyed two Bf 109s to become an ace, having claimed all of his victories since D-Day. Leading the section was Flt Lt 'Gordie' Troke, who also bagged a pair to claim his final victories. As they departed the area Spitfires

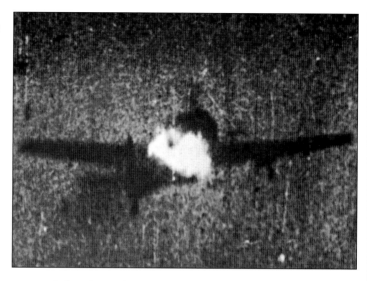

from No 412 Sqn arrived over Nijmegen and shot down three more fighters to the east of the town, one falling to Flg Off David Jamieson for his eighth kill. As one squadron diarist wrote, 'it had been one heck of a morning!'

The action was not yet done, however, as shortly before midday it was No 416 Sqn's turn when eight-victory ace Flt Lt Jake Mitchner, on his first trip with his new unit, led 12 Spitfires on another low patrol over the Nijmegen-Emmerich area. There, they joined in a large dogfight between 20 Fw 190s and some Tempest Vs, claiming a further seven victories. Every time Mitchner tried to get on the tail of an enemy aircraft another appeared on his tail, but he quickly turned the tables and, with a short burst, sent one of the Fw 190s down in flames. He then attacked a second machine, seeing its hood fly off and the pilot leap

from his flame-filled cockpit. Amongst others to enjoy success was Flt Lt Neil Russell, who was led a merry chase by an Fw 190 before he was able to get his sights on his quarry. The enemy fighter was rocked by a large explosion as a result of his fire, and it blew up upon hitting the bank of a river. This aircraft was Russell's fourth, and final, victory.

After the bloodletting of previous days, the month ended relatively quietly, although German jets were again in evidence as No 441 Sqn's Flt Lt Ron Lake hit an Me 262 near Nijmegen shortly before noon. A little later No 416's Sqn Ldr John McElroy was leading another patrol over the Nijmegen bridge when a bomb-carrying Fw 190 with an escorting Bf 109 was spotted. He broke onto the latter's tail and the enemy pilot released his drop tank as he hit the Messerschmitt, leaving the fighter streaming glycol. Flt Lt Dave Harling also targeted the Bf 109, catching it with several more bursts that caused the pilot to pull up vertically and then bail out. This shared victory made Harling 2nd TAF's latest ace, and it signalled the end

to No 416 Sqn's most productive period of aerial action. It was also McElroy's last success in World War 2, although he was to gain three further victories flying for the Israelis in 1948, two of which were, ironically, RAF Spitfires.

October ushered in some of the worst autumnal weather on record that in turn had a profound effect on air operations, causing frequent disruptions and making living conditions at forward airfields intolerable. Nonetheless, when conditions were suitable there continued to be significant engagements fought between 2nd TAF fighters and a still formidable Luftwaffe. Proof of the latter point came on 2 October when, during a patrol by No 416 Sqn over Nijmegen, five-victory ace Flt Lt Russ Bouskill was killed in combat with Fw 190s of II./JG 26. Jets still continued to be found too, and that day Flg Off Forrest Young of No 442 Sqn engaged an Me 262 near Cleve. In a head-on attack he saw his fire hit the enemy's wing. Three days later came a cause for some rejoicing.

During a sweep over Holland on 5 October, 12 Spitfire IXs from No 401 Sqn had yet another encounter with an Me 262. Led by unit CO Sqn Ldr Rod Smith, the RCAF pilots were flying aircraft that had by now all been fitted with the latest gyro gunsights. These would prove to be highly effective in combat against the considerably faster Messerschmitt. At 1430 hrs near Nijmegen, No 401 Sqn spotted Me 262 '9K+BL' of 5./KG 51, flown by Hauptmann Hans-Christoph Buttmann. Smith subsequently wrote in his combat report;

'I was leading No 401 Sqn at 13,000 ft in the Nijmegen area about five miles northeast of the bridge. We were flying on a north-easterly course when I sighted an Me 262 head-on 500 ft below us. He went into a port climbing turn and I turned to starboard after him, along with several other Spitfires. He then dived down towards the bridge, twisting, turning and half-rolling at very high speed. He then flew across Nijmegen, turning from side to side. I saw a Spitfire get some strikes on him and he streamed white

Spitfire IXs of No 412 Sqn are seen here dispersed at B84 Rips in October 1944. The nearest aircraft is thought to be Mk IX NH258/VZ-N, in which Flt Lt Charlie Fox had made a damaged claim for an Fw 190 on 20 August. By year-end his tally stood at four destroyed and five damaged. Frustratingly for Fox, he saw no further aerial action after 29 December (*DND*)

smoke from the starboard wing root. He flew on at very high speed nevertheless, and I managed to get behind him and fire two three-second bursts from approximately 200-300 yards. He zoomed very high and I saw strikes on him in the port and starboard nacelles. A small fire started in the starboard nacelle and a big one in the port nacelle while I was firing. I broke down to starboard under him and he turned down to starboard behind me. I thought at the time he was trying to attack me, even though in flames. He passed behind me and crashed in a field southwest of Nijmegen.'

Others from the section that had also attacked Buttmann's jet were future 13-victory ace Flg Off John MacKay, Flg Off Gus Sinclair (this being the latter's fourth, and last, success) and Flt Lts 'Snooks' Everard and 'Tex' Davenport. The latter pilot, having avoided a near collision with his CO's Spitfire, eventually opened fire, as he later explained;

'I finally closed in to 300 yards line astern and emptied the remainder of my guns – approximately 10 or 12 seconds – into the kite, observing strikes in both engines and the fuselage. The aircraft was burning all this time. The pilot seemed to be unhurt, and put up a good fight during this action.'

The unfortunate Buttmann, who was killed when he bailed out too low, had tangled with a very experienced and able team. Davenport's shared final claim took him to acedom. More significantly, this was the first jet to be shot down by a Commonwealth squadron.

## DEADLY FLAK

The Luftwaffe maintained its high tempo of operations over the Dutch-German border on 6 October. No 442 Sqn had a heavy engagement with around 100 enemy fighters, resulting in Flt Lt Stan McClarty's formation claiming three victories, including a Bf 109 that he shot down. In another fight near Cleve the following day Flg Off Forrest Young shot down a brace of Fw 190s to take his total to four, but a month later debris from a train he was attacking hit his aircraft and he bailed out to become a PoW, having failed to claim his fifth victory.

A combination of bad weather and recent exertions then led to something of a hiatus in aerial fighting. As Allied ground forces consolidated and prepared to push toward the Rhine, most Spitfire squadrons concentrated on ground attack, with the resultant steady stream of losses mainly to the ever deadly light flak. Typical of the units to see action at this time were the Kiwis of No 485 Sqn that flew a daily round of ground attack missions, as described to the author by six-victory ace Flt Lt Owen Hardy;

'The Germans used cover to assemble infantry before mounting a counter attack, but our forces indicated the position by red smoke from mortar or artillery shells. Our Spitfires then swept down, ignoring the flak, and ruined their plans with a barrage of cannon fire.'

There was a brief upsurge of aerial combat at the end of October such as on the 28th when, in the early afternoon, No 412 Sqn's Flt Lt Don Laubman shot down two Fw 190s of II./JG 26 over Hohenbudberg, one of which was flown by Oberfeldwebel Karl-Heinz Knobeloch, to take his total to 16. These victories made Laubman the most successful Spitfire pilot of the Northwest Europe campaign. Two hours later his squadronmate Flt Lt Phil Charron shot down two Bf 109s of III./JG 26 near Altenberge to take his final score to seven.

With the Luftwaffe having now withdrawn its units to airfields within Germany, most Fighter Command squadrons switched to escort duties. In early November Wg Cdr Bobby Oxspring arrived to lead the Detling Wing, which was comprised of Sqn Ldr Pat Lardner-Burke's No 1 Sqn and No 165 under newly arrived Sqn Ldr Jas Storrar. The latter, who was already an ace, was described as being 'unflappable' by Oxspring. Storrar flew his first operation as CO in Spitfire IX MK242/SK-A from Detling on a mission to Homburg on 8 November.

Leading the Harrowbeer Wing aloft (in Spitfire IX in MJ845/HBW) that same day was Wg Cdr Harold 'Birdy' Bird-Wilson.

To give UK-based Spitfires the necessary range to reach western Germany the aircraft were fitted with cumbersome 45-gallon overload tanks. However, with the Bomber Command 'heavies' generally flying as a stream rather than in formation, these missions presented the escorts with many problems. The most frequent targets were in the Ruhr valley, and although interference from the Luftwaffe was the exception, flak was always heavy, as Oxspring recalled;

'Flying several thousand feet above our charges, we, with our constant manoeuvrings, were not specifically targeted. But it was inspiring to witness the guts of the bomber crews as, concentrating on their bombing runs, they drove undeviating into the lethal defensive curtain.'

At the end of the month John McElroy finished his tour and was replaced as CO of No 416 Sqn by fellow ace Sqn Ldr Jake Mitchner. Also joining the unit for a fresh tour was Flt Lt John 'Webb' Harten, who already had three victories to his name. Armed reconnaissance patrols were the order of the day as the Anglo-Canadian 21st Army Group pushed toward the German border. Enemy fighters continued to be seen, and during a dive-bombing attack near Coesfeld on 2 November a section from No 442 Sqn spotted four Fw 190s. In the subsequent engagement Flt Lt Milt Jowsey (flying Spitfire IX MJ463/Y2-K) shot one of them down for his fifth victory – he had previously achieved four victories in the Mediterranean. A second fighter was destroyed by Flg Off John Francis, who was on his very first operational sortie. He eventually made seven claims, including four destroyed.

Forty-eight hours after this action No 416 Sqn moved into B56 Evere, on the outskirts of Brussels, where pilots were accommodated in what they described as 'a beautiful home in Boulevard General Wahis'.

Amongst the Spitfire units on the Continent at this time was No 127 Sqn at B60 Grimbergen, just north of Brussels. On 30 October it lost three aircraft to flak, with one pilot killed and another wounded – the latter was the CO, Sqn Ldr F W Lister. He was replaced by Czech

Flt Lt Phil Charron of No 412 Sqn was one of many RCAF Spitfire pilots to 'make ace' following the invasion. He lost his life on 19 November after leading his section of four Spitfires into action against more than 40 German fighters from II./JG 26. Three of the four Spitfires were shot down and two pilots killed (*DND*)

ace Sqn Ldr Otto Smik, described by a contemporary as 'a very affable chap'. Smik flew his first mission (in newly delivered Spitfire XVI RR227) on 18 November when he escorted Mitchells sent to bomb Viersen.

The following afternoon No 412 Sqn was out on a dive-bombing mission that ran into 40 marauding Fw 190s of 5./JG 26, led by Leutnant Richard Vogt, that shot down three Spitfires. One was flown by seven-victory ace Flt Lt Phil Charron, who was killed.

Despite such losses patrols and sweeps over northern Germany and Holland continued at a ferocious pace, with rail and road traffic being targeted predominately. On 26 November, after attacking vehicles on a bridge near the Dutch border town of Venlo, Flg Off Fred Murray of No 412 Sqn began his path to acedom when he shot down an Fw 190 – he reported seeing smoke and flame emanating from the cockpit as it rolled over and crashed. Attacking another bridge at Zwolle two days later, No 127 Sqn lost two Spitfire XVIs to flak. Both pilots were killed, one of whom was the CO, Sqn Ldr Otto Smik. He was succeeded by Sqn Ldr 'Sammy' Sampson, who was impressed with his new mount, particularly when it came to aerial combat;

'The Spitfire IX/XVI was now fitted with a gyroscopic gunsight – a very sophisticated piece of machinery. When the sight was switched on there were some 12 small graticules that could be moved by turning the grip on the throttle, which could be twisted. At 800 yards the graticules sat on the inside edge of the sight, and by twisting the grip these could be moved away from the centre, where they stopped at 100 yards range. In the centre of the sight was a fixed cross, and in addition there was a movable "dot". The object when entering combat with the enemy was to get the movable dot onto the fixed cross, and this would occur if you were approaching in line astern. The sight also took into account speed, slip and skid.'

Sampson's new squadron formed part of No 132 (Norwegian) Wing, which was commanded by successful nightfighter pilot Gp Capt Douglas 'Zulu' Morris, with Norwegian ace Lt Col Rolf Berg as Wing Leader.

Rain, with its accompanying low cloud or fog, continued to affect air activity, particularly at low level, into December, and under its cover the Germans were assembling a new offensive in the Ardennes. When out dive-bombing railways near Wesel on the 5th No 412 Sqn spotted a large formation of Bf 109s (probably from JG 27) at medium level, and in the ensuing fight eight-victory ace Flt Lt Wilfred Banks hit two that he could only claim as 'probables', although future ace Flt Lt Fred Murray shot down two. Elsewhere that day, during a bomber escort, Flg Off J A Faulkner of Manston-based No 91 Sqn destroyed a Bf 109. However, his squadronmate, and V1 ace, Flg Off Ken Collier was killed in combat with Bf 109s over Hamm.

On 6 December the Supreme Headquarters Allied Expeditionary Force (the headquarters of the Commander of Allied forces in Northwest Europe) issued Operational Memorandum No 23, ordering distinctive markings to be removed from all aircraft

A close-up of the new GM2 gyro gunsight, which was fitted to the Spitfire from late 1944. A major step forward in air-to-air gunnery, the gunsight gave the 'average' fighter pilot a much better chance of scoring hits and making kills. It was used to good effect when the pilots of No 401 Sqn shot down the first Me 262 on 5 October 1944, and Flt Lt Dick Audet also praised the GM2 after he claimed his five victories in just a matter of minutes on 29 December (*Donald Nijboer*)

Pilots of No 411 Sqn enjoy a break in the sunshine at B80 Volkel in October 1944. Seated on the left is future ace Flt Lt John Boyle, who shot down an Me 262 on Christmas Day, whilst next to him is Flg Off Denny Wilson, who eventually became an ace flying for the Israelis in 1948 when his fifth victim, somewhat ironically, was an Egyptian Spitfire. The remaining two pilots are Flg Off A C McNiece and Flt Lt R A Gilberstad, who claimed one destroyed and one damaged (*PAC*)

except photo-reconnaissance Mosquitoes and Spitfires from 31 December, thus obliterating the last vestiges of the D-Day markings. Two days later No 442 Sqn began operations from B88 Heesch, and some of its Spitfire XVIs somewhat optimistically chased three Me 262s.

Elsewhere, Nos 403 and 416 Sqns flew two sweeps, attacking ground targets. On the second of these, near Wesel, a trio of Bf 109s was spotted, one of which was shot down by Flt Lt Liv Foster of No 403 Sqn. Another was seen about three miles away by No 416 Sqn's CO, Jake Mitchner, who quickly overhauled the Messerschmitt and followed it through a series of increasingly desperate turns as the enemy pilot tried to shake him off. Eventually, Mitchner managed to get close enough and fire off a brief burst, after which the Bf 109 went straight in and crashed on its back in a field. It was the last of his 10.5 victories.

The weather improved enough on 14 December to allow the Luftwaffe to mount more than 100 fighter sorties. One element was engaged by No 412 Sqn, whose pilots shot down two aircraft to become 2nd TAF's top-scoring unit. Later that same day No 442 Sqn's CO, Sqn Ldr Bill Olmstead, had to bail out over Grave when his fighter was hit by flak during an attack on a rail target near Groenlo. Although he was promptly returned to 2nd TAF, Olmstead was replaced by ace Sqn Ldr Milt Jowsey.

At dawn on the 16th, under the cover of deteriorating winter weather, the Germans launched a counter offensive in the Ardennes that became known as the Battle of the Bulge. The offensive had the Belgian city of Liege as its initial objective, followed by the vital port of Antwerp. Despite the weather, Allied squadrons flew whenever they could to try to blunt the enemy thrust, particularly by interdicting the vulnerable supply routes. Whenever conditions improved there would be an upsurge in aerial combat and losses to ground fire. One of the few Merlin-engined Spitfire units to make any claims during this period was No 66 Sqn, which on the 18th shot down a Bf 109 over Cologne and damaged four more.

On Christmas Eve the weather that had covered the German advance in the Ardennes suddenly lifted, allowing Allied fighters to swarm into the air in order to blunt the offensive.

During the day the tactical reconnaissance Spitfire IXs of No 414 Sqn flew 36 sorties. Shortly before midday near the town of Krefeld, the unit's Flt Lt 'Sammy' Hall, who had been monitoring the condition of bridges and movement of enemy transport, came across 15 Bf 109s. In the brief fight that ensued he shot two of them down. In the outstanding combat of the day, Hall had downed two *experte*, namely Hauptmann Erich Woitke, *Gruppenkommandeur* of III./JG 1, who was a Spanish Civil War veteran with 29 victories, and five-victory ace Leutnant Hubert Heckmann.

Then, near Cologne, at 1535 hrs another section of No 414 Sqn fighters led by Flt Lt Bill Sawers (in Mk IX MJ966/J) was bounced by 12 Bf 109s from IV./JG 27. Quickly turning the tables in a quite remarkable combat, Sawers shot down three of them and damaged two more. During the afternoon, however, four Spitfire XVIs of No 416 Sqn were shot down in error by US Army anti-aircraft fire and one of the pilots was killed. Later that same day, during another afternoon patrol, a second No 416 Sqn pilot was killed by American guns when he fell victim to a USAAF P-47.

Returning to his base at B88 Heesch on 25 December after completing an uneventful sweep, future ace Flt Lt Jack Boyle of No 411 Sqn got a wonderful Christmas present when he spotted an Me 262 attacking the airfield. Diving after the jet at more than 500 mph, he opened fire at long range and hit its port engine, which started to stream smoke. Boyle quickly caught up with the crippled aircraft, and firing again he watched 9K+MM of II./KG 51, flown by Oberleutnant Hans-Georg Lamle, crash in flames near Erfstadt, southwest of Cologne.

Several hours later No 401 Sqn departed B88 Heesch on a sweep that saw the unit engage Bf 109s of *Stab*/JG 77, two of which were shot down. One of these was the second success for Flg Off John MacKay, the fighter crashing into the suburbs of the shattered city of Duisburg. However, debris from one of the Messerschmitts hit Sqn Ldr Hedley Everard's aircraft and he was forced to bail out near Venlo and was captured.

Then, just as dusk was falling, 12 Spitfire XVIs from No 403 Sqn, led by Sqn Ldr Jim Collier, found a *Kette* of three Me 262s flying in large

Through the winter of 1944-45 most 2nd TAF Spitfire squadrons performed fighter-bomber missions. One was No 74 Sqn, to which Spitfire IX PV144/4D-A belonged – it is seen here bombed up at B70 Deurne, near Antwerp, in late 1944. This fighter was the usual mount of the CO, five-victory ace Sqn Ldr Jim Hayter (*M J F Bowyer*)

circles southwest of Aachen. As the RCAF fighters approached two of the jets made off, but the third one, 9K+MK of I./KG 51 flown by Feldwebel Hans Meyer, continued circling, apparently unaware of the impending threat. As Collier came within range he opened fire, seeing strikes on one wing. The jet then attempted to escape but Collier tenaciously maintained position and continued to fire, seeing smoke begin to stream from its left engine. The jet rolled onto its back and the pilot bailed out near Liège. Collier's notable victory was his fifth claim, of which three were destroyed.

More jets were seen on 26 December, as Sqn Ldr 'Sammy' Sampson of No 127 Sqn recalled;

'On Boxing Day we saw some Hun aircraft during a sortie into the Enschede area. There were some jet jobs reported and then we saw four Me 262s, but we had no hope of catching them. I had a long-range squirt from 1500 yards, but more in desperation than with any sense of hitting one.'

Wg Cdr Ray Harries, No 135 Wing's Wing Leader, was more fortunate though when escorting bombers over the Ardennes, for he managed to damage one – it would prove to be the high-scoring ace's final claim.

There was little aerial action for the 2nd TAF fighter units over the next two days, but that changed on the 29th when one of the most remarkable Spitfire combats of the war took place. The first significant action involved No 331 Sqn, led by Maj Martin Gran, which shot down four of III./JG 54's new 'long nosed' Fw 190Ds – one of these fell to the ace CO. However, four Spitfires were also lost. An RAF contemporary said of Gran;

'I consider him to be the bravest of the brave. He was leading his squadron on 29 December on an armed reconnaissance at 4000 ft, adjacent to the clutch of German occupied airfields of Henglo, Almelo and Enschede, when some eight Me 109s and FW 190s took off in a hurry, but still as a unit. They must have been aware of the Norge Squadron, for they were turning very hard to port when they were engaged – so much so that it was, as Martin later said, impossible to get the dot onto the cross on his gunsight. He then told me that he had to apply what he had been taught at the Central Gunnery School – pull through the target and start firing short bursts when the target was out of sight. He managed this against three of the fighters, which left two ME 109s and one FW 190 burning on the ground. He got a bar to his DFC for this effort.'

Aside from his Fw 190D, Martin Gran was also credited with two Bf 109s destroyed, whilst the rest of his squadron claimed nine more. Capt Helner Grundt-Spang shot down three of them to take his score to ten, with two more falling to the fire of Lt Ragnar Dogger to take him to acedom. Also elevated to this status was 2Lt Ola Aanjesen, who shot down another Bf 109. A short while later Flt Lt Fred Murray of No 401 Sqn shot down an Fw 190 near Rheine to claim his third victory. Also successful was squadronmate Flt Lt Gregory 'Cam' Cameron, who also destroyed a Focke-Wulf to begin his path to acedom.

Impressive though all this was, the outstanding combat of the day belonged to No 411 Sqn. Patrolling northeast of Osnabrück, the Canadians initially spotted a lone Me 262 before seeing a mixed formation of enemy fighters below and off to the right of it at the 'two o'clock' position. Leading the Spitfires in Mk IX RR201/DB-G was 22-year-old Flt Lt Dick Audet, who, having initially been retained in Canada as an

instructor, had spent much of his time in England flying with an anti-aircraft cooperation unit. Finally posted to No 411 Sqn in September 1944, Audet had not yet met any German aircraft in combat. Leading his section down, he described the remarkable events that followed in his combat report;

'I attacked an Me 109 that was the last aircraft in the formation of about 12, all flying line astern. At approximately 200 yards and 30 degrees to starboard, and at a height of 10,000 ft, I opened fire and saw strikes all over the fuselage and wing roots. The Me 109 burst into flames on the starboard side of the fuselage only, trailing intense black smoke. I then broke off my attack.

'After the first attack I went around in a defensive circle at about 8500 ft until I spotted an Fw 190 that I immediately attacked from 250 yards down to 100 yards and from 30 degrees to line astern. I saw strikes over the cockpit and to the rear of the fuselage. It burst into flames from the engine back, and as I passed very close over the top of it I saw the pilot slumped over in the cockpit, which was also in flames.

'My third attack followed immediately after the second. I followed what I believed was a Me 109 in a slight dive. He then climbed sharply and his canopy flew off at about 3000-4000 ft. I then gave a very short burst from about 300 yards and line astern and his aircraft whipped downwards in a dive. The pilot attempted or did bail out. I saw a black object on the edge of the cockpit but his 'chute was ripped to shreds. I then took cine shots of his aircraft going to the ground and the bits of parachute floating around. I saw this aircraft hit and smash into many flaming pieces on the ground. I do not remember any strikes on his aircraft. The Browning button only may have been pressed.

'I spotted an Fw 190 being pursued at about 5000 ft by a Spitfire that was in turn pursued by an Fw 190. I called this Yellow section pilot to

**Possibly the most dramatic combat of the campaign was flown by Flt Lt Dick Audet of No 411 Sqn who, in his first ever aerial combat, on 29 December shot down three Fw 190s and two Bf 109s to thus become an 'ace in a sortie'. In all, he was credited with 11 victories, including an Me 262, before he was lost to flak while strafing a train on 3 March 1945 (DND)**

Audet's aircraft on his remarkable sortie was Spitfire IX RR201, although it then wore the codes DB-G. After servicing and being re-coded as DB-R, as seen here, it was used by Flg Off Denny Wilson to shoot down a He 111 on 16 April 1945, thus starting him on his path to acedom (*PAC*)

break and attacked the Fw 190 up his rear. The fight went downwards in a steep dive. When I was about 250 yards line astern of this Fw 190 I opened fire. There were many strikes on the length of the fuselage, and it immediately burst into flames. I saw this Fw 190 go straight into the ground and burn.

'Several minutes later, while attempting to form my section up again, I spotted an Fw 190 from 4000 ft. He was about 2000 ft below me, so I dived down on him and he turned in to me from the right. Then he flipped around in a left hand turn and attempted a head-on attack. I slowed down to wait for the Fw 190 to fly into range. At about 200 yards and 20 degrees I gave a very short burst, but couldn't see any strikes. This aircraft flicked violently, and continued to do so until it crashed into the ground. The remainder of my section saw this encounter, and "Yellow 4" saw it crash in flames.'

Dick Audet had become an ace in the space of two minutes. This was also the only occasion that a Spitfire pilot shot down five aircraft in a single sortie.

The momentous year ended on a successful note for the Spitfire units, which claimed a further seven victories on 31 December. Near Rheine just before midday No 411 Sqn's Flt Lt Jack Boyle shot down a Ju 88, while his wingman Flg Off Malcolm Graham destroyed a long-nosed Fw 190D. These successes provided both future aces with their third victories. Returning from an armed reconnaissance, No 442 Sqn intercepted more than a dozen Bf 109s near Münster and brought down four of them. One fell to Flt Lt Don Pieri, a Texan who, with Flt Lt Perkins, chased and harried his opponent until it crashed into a small hill. This was the American's first success on his way to acedom. The year had thus ended well for No 442 Sqn, these victories taking its total to 31 since D-Day.

As dusk fell the last Merlin Spitfire victory of the year fell to Flg Off Tapley of No 416 Sqn when he shot down an Fw 190.

# INTO THE REICH

'The New Year started with a bang'. Thus with splendid understatement did the No 401 Sqn diarist note the last great offensive undertaken by the Luftwaffe, codenamed Operation *Bodenplatte*. Weeks in the planning, as dawn broke on 1 January 1945 2nd TAF airfields in Belgium, Holland and northern France came under attack as waves of almost 1000 German fighters swept over them in an attempt to deliver a knock out blow and wrench air superiority from the Allies. However, *Bodenplatte* was to have the reverse effect, for German casualties were heavy and included many experienced veterans that it could ill afford.

The day fighter waves were led by Ju 88G nightfighters, the enemy hoping to catch 2nd TAF on the ground. They were to be disappointed, however, as some Allied squadrons were already airborne on sweeps themselves.

At B65 Maldeghem the Bf 109G-14s of III./JG 1 arrived a little after 0900 hrs, and although No 349 Sqn escaped almost unscathed, its Kiwi neighbours in No 485 Sqn were not so lucky, losing 11 Spitfire IXs destroyed and two more badly damaged. The personal aircraft of No 135 Wing Wing Leader, Wg Cdr Ray Harries, was also written off. Over at B61 St Denis-Westrem, the three Polish squadrons of No 131 Wing had left on early morning missions, as had tactical reconnaissance flights by the Spitfire IXs of No 34 Wing based at B58 Melsbroek.

At B78 Eindhoven, the CO of No 414 Sqn, Sqn Ldr Gordon Wonnacott (who had previously claimed three victories when flying Mustang Is) was returning to base following a patrol when, at 0930 hrs, he saw German fighters strafing. He promptly went after them and, near the town of Helmond, shot down a Bf 109 and two Fw 190s – one of the latter machines was probably flown by Unteroffizier Gerhard Schmidt of 3./JG 3. This haul took Wonnacott to ace status in some style. The first pilot to reach acedom in 1945 was awarded an immediate bar to his DFC for the exploit.

At B88 Heesch some Spitfires had already departed when, at 0900 hrs, just as No 401 Sqn was lining up for takeoff, more than 40 enemy fighters flew over the strip. Flg Off 'Cam' Cameron quickly scrambled into the clear winter sky, accelerating after a pair of Bf 109s. He hit the right hand aircraft near the cockpit and it nosed over into the ground. As it did so he fired on the second Messerschmitt, which he set on fire. Spotting a third fighter off to his right, Cameron chased it and opened fire from 400 yards. Seeing hits on the engine and glycol coolant streaming back from the stricken aircraft, he watched it crash land in a field just outside the aerodrome. Cameron landed back at Heesch just ten minutes later. He became an ace in late April.

Squadronmate Flt Lt John MacKay was up in Spitfire IX MH240/YO-Z, and his section was directed towards the Reichwald Forest. Here, spotting a Focke-Wulf at very low level, he dived on the evading fighter. As he straightened MacKay fired a killing burst that caused the Fw 190 to explode and crash in flames. Now separated from his section near

Nijmegen, he saw an Fw 190 on the tail of a Tempest V. Although he subsequently ran out of ammunition, MacKay got so close to the tail of his opponent that the German pilot clipped an ice-covered lake with his wingtip and crashed. As he pulled up, MacKay ran straight into a Bf 109. Manoeuvring onto its tail, he again forced his quarry into such desperate evasion at very low level that the fighter struck trees and crashed. The aggressive flying by 23-year-old MacKay resulted in him becoming an ace in spectacular fashion – and earned him the immediate award of a DFC.

Having taken off on an armed reconnaissance with No 411 Sqn shortly before *Bodenplatte*, Flt Lt Dick Audet spotted an Fw 190 below him near B106 Twente and dived after it. Although the enemy pilot pulled into a sharp turn to the right, Audet opened fire and hit the Focke-Wulf hard. The fighter rolled over and spun down in flames until it crashed. Climbing back up, Audet then spotted a second Fw 190. Getting in behind it, he opened fire and saw pieces fly off the fuselage and rudder. The fighter's engine then stopped, allowing Audet to close in and attack it for a second time. The enemy aircraft dived into the ground east of Haarsdergen moments later.

No 442 Sqn had also taken off before B88 Heesch was targeted, the unit being recalled once the attack had commenced. Near Venlo, the squadron ran into some of the returning enemy fighters, and brought five of them down. Despite his rough-running engine, Flt Lt Donald 'Chunky' Gordon fired a deflection shot from 200 yards at the first Fw 190 that he encountered and watched it immediately flick to the left and crash into the ground. He then banked to the left and went after a second Focke-Wulf, firing a burst from 300 yards and seeing strikes before it too crashed into the ground and blew up. Then a burst of anti-aircraft fire wounded Gordon in the head, neck and back, forcing him to crash land in Allied territory. Once on the ground an excited Dutch woman rushed up to him in the cockpit to wish him a Happy New Year! In hospital doctors removed no fewer than 17 pieces of shrapnel from his body. Gordon's elevation to acedom had been hard won, as was his immediate DFC.

Hearing Gordon's R/T calls, others headed back to Heesch and shot down a few more Fw 190s. Two of these fell to Flt Lt Don Pieri, so moving him a little closer to acedom.

During the morning attacks the Spitfire squadrons were credited with 47 victories – more than any other type – with the honours going to the three Polish squadrons, which claimed 20 of them. Anti-aircraft fire and crashes had also taken a significant toll on the Luftwaffe, which lost more than 270 aircraft in total. Its future effectiveness would suffer as a result of these losses. *Bodenplatte* had not been one-sided, however, as the No 416 Sqn archives described;

'At the time the enemy aircraft roared down on Evere several of No 416 Sqn's Spitfires were taxiing out to take off on a sweep. Before they could leave the runway three of them were shot up and damaged. Only Flt Lt David Harling was able to get airborne. Single-handedly, he engaged the enemy over Brussels and was shot down and killed. Courage, keenness and devotion to duty even unto death.'

After the events of the morning, for most of the Spitfire wings it was soon back to 'business as usual'. At around midday No 74 Sqn, led by the desert ace Flt Lt Dennis Usher, and No 345 Sqn, led by Cne Louis Lemaire from

As German fighters swept over B56 Evere on their New Year's Day attack Flt Lt Dave Harling of No 416 Sqn took off alone to counter them, but the ace was overwhelmed and shot down by Bf 109s of JG 26 (*No 416 Sqn*)

On 1 January No 412 Sqn's CO Sqn Ldr Dean Dover shot down a Bf 109 and shared an Fw 190 to become an ace. He is seen here having a celebratory drink with the commander of No 126 Wing, Gp Capt Gordon McGregor, who was the oldest RCAF fighter pilot to see combat during World War 2 (*Canadian Forces*)

No 145 (French) Wing, escorted USAAF B-26s sent to attack targets near Trier. Enemy forces had begun withdrawing from positions south of Malmedy as the Ardennes fighting began to swing back in favour of the Allies, thanks in no small part to the efforts of 2nd TAF units.

During an armed reconnaissance to the Dortmund area on 1 January Flt Lt Wilfred Banks of No 412 Sqn found a lone Ju 88 that he quickly despatched to claim his ninth, and last, kill. At 1515 hrs his CO, Sqn Ldr Dean Dover, led a sweep to Osnabrück. At 12,000 ft near Gütersloh he spotted a pair of Bf 109s, and diving on them opened fire from 400 yards, seeing hits on the left wing of one of the fighters. As it turned, Dover closed in to about 50 yards before firing a two-second burst. He observed more strikes all over its wings and fuselage before the Bf 109 flicked over and crashed into the ground, elevating him to acedom. Dover's wingman bagged the second Messerschmitt.

Two more RCAF Spitfire pilots became aces three days later when, in the early afternoon of 4 January, No 411 Sqn was conducting an armed reconnaissance in the Henglo area of eastern Holland. The unit engaged a formation of Fw 190s, possibly from I./JG 1, and shot down six of them. Flg Off Malcolm Graham got two whilst Flt Lt Jack Boyle got one and shared a second, making both pilots aces.

Escorting daylight raids by heavy bombers continued to occupy British-based Spitfire squadrons in the New Year, and despite the bitter winter weather such missions continued unabated. No 1 Sqn's new CO, eight-victory ace Sqn Ldr David Cox, recalled some of the sorties that he flew at this time;

Battle of Britain veteran Sqn Ldr David Cox, who had become an ace over North Africa in 1942, led No 1 Sqn on escort missions for Bomber Command 'heavies' performing daylight raids on Germany in 1945 (*D G S R Cox*)

Groundcrew survey flak damage to the tail of Spitfire IX PV213/AH-W of No 332 Sqn at B79 Woensdrecht. Flying it on 14 January 1945, Capt Kaare Bolstad shot down an Me 262 for his second, and last, victory (*Bengt Stangvik*)

'One of the longest penetrations we did was to Paderborn, well into Germany. Another was to Mannheim – very picturesque, with snow on the ground. Of course we had 90-gallon drop tanks, but we would also refuel in Belgium or Holland, usually at either Maldeghem or Ursel.'

German jets continued to be regularly encountered, but their performance meant that they could only be successfully engaged in the most favourable of circumstances. On 14 January the Luftwaffe lost almost 180 aircraft, the majority to Eighth Air Force escort fighters, but 2nd TAF Spitfires also contributed 17 confirmed claims. Several aces increased their scores, with the outstanding figure on the day being No 411 Sqn's Flt Lt Johnny MacKay, as the unit diarist excitedly wrote;

'Great joy experienced by the squadron, which caught a number of FW 190s taking off and landing on Twente aerodrome. The squadron attacked immediately, and five FW 190s were shot down and destroyed. Flt Lt J MacKay destroyed three!'

Another fell to Flt Lt Fred Murray, whose final confirmed victory made him an ace. In fact I./JG 1 lost six Fw 190s over Twente, No 411 Sqn's likely victims being Unteroffizier Hans Heidrich (flying Wk-Nr 739235/ White 5), Obergefreiter Walter Mämpel, Oberfähnrich Helmut Schager, Feldwebel Otto Schiltz (in Wk-Nr 960217/Black 2), Oberfeldwebel Gerhard Kühl (in Green 21) and Unteroffizier Wolfgang Kindshaüser (in Red 4).

Mid-afternoon that same day No 132 Wing's two Norwegian squadrons, Nos 331 and 332, flew a sweep over the Osnabrück area, meeting large formations of piston-engined fighters and several jets near Rheine airfield. No 332 Sqn dived on several of the latter, and Capt Kaare Bolstad (in Mk IX PV213/AH-W) shot down Me 262 9K+LP of 6./KG 51 flown by Unteroffizier Friedrich Christoph, who was killed. Five Fw 190s and Bf 109s also fell, one of the latter being claimed by No 331 Sqn's CO, Maj Martin Gran, as his tenth, and last, success. Also claiming his final kill was fellow ace Capt Helner Grundt-Spang.

Jets were also encountered by the bomber escort units, as Wg Cdr Bobby Oxspring recalled;

'In a despairing show of defiance to a raid on Essen, the Luftwaffe pumped up a pair of Me 262s high above the bomber stream. It was the first time we'd seen the much-vaunted German jets. We jettisoned our external tanks and prepared for battle, but they declined to engage and disappeared at high speed. The final glimpse I had of the Luftwaffe was a solitary Messerschmitt 163 rocket-powered delta fighter, which, leaving a long black trail, climbed at astonishing speed into a formation of Lancasters. Before we could cut it off it fired, but missed, and screamed away into the stratosphere, not to be seen again.'

It was not all success though, as German flak was no respecter of air fighting reputation. No 485 Sqn's Flt Lt Allen Stead, who had 14 claims to his name (including four destroyed), was shot down and killed when the dummy train he attacked 'exploded' with anti aircraft fire – ironically, he should have finished his tour some time earlier. On 17 January No 127 Sqn's Flt Lt Clive 'Jumbo' Birbeck was on an armed reconnaissance to Maasluis when his fighter was hit by flak and he was forced to bail out at Overflakee. Three days later No 412 Sqn lost four more aircraft to flak in the Münster area. Three pilots became PoWs but one evaded. There was a great loss on 3 February when the

Capt Helner Grundt-Spang was one of the leading Norwegian aces, and on 29 December he shot down three Bf 109s. His 11th, and last, victory came on 14 January when he shot down an Fw 190 near Osnabrück during an armed reconnaissance mission (*Bengt Stangvik*)

successful Norwegian leader of No 132 Wing, Wg Cdr Rolf Berg, was shot down and killed by flak attacking an airfield in Holland. Another Norwegian loss was Maj Kaare Bolstad, who, having become CO of No 332 Sqn on 28 February, was shot down and killed by flak near Zwolle whilst strafing on 3 April.

Before January was out more jets had been claimed. During an armed reconnaissance over Lingen and Münster on the 23rd Flt Lt Dick Audet, again flying RR201, was near Rheine at 1215 hrs when he destroyed an Me 262 on the ground. Five minutes later he spotted another jet in the air attempting to land, and he promptly shot it down too – this aircraft was possibly the aircraft flown by Unteroffizier Kubizek of 4./KG 51. This was Audet's 11th, and final, victory, all of which had been achieved in less than a month.

Earlier that same day No 401 Sqn had also found some jets when, near Berg, at 1030 hrs they attacked Arado Ar 234 bombers of 9./KG 76 flown by Oberfeldwebel Uhlmann, Unteroffizier Sienhold and Oberleutnant Kolm. The successful pilots were Flt Lt Don Church and Flg Off G A Hardy, with Plt Off M Thomas and Flt Lt William 'Bud' Connell sharing the third jet. The latter thus took his total to four destroyed. The CO, Sqn Ldr Bill Klersy, also damaged an Ar 234 in the air, whilst Flt Lt Fred Murray damaged several more Arados on the ground at Braunsche airfield.

23 January also saw another hectic day's aerial fighting in the Lippstadt area, with No 421 Sqn being in action against Fw 190Ds. The unit CO, Sqn Ldr John Browne, claimed his fourth victory when he shot down one of them, with another Focke-Wulf being shared by Flg Off Evans and Flt Lt Malcolm 'Mac' Gordon, the share making the latter pilot an ace.

No 145 Wing's new Wing Leader, Wg Cdr Sammy Sampson, undertook his first mission with the unit on the 23rd;

The leader of No 145 (French) Wing, Wg Cdr 'Sammy' Sampson, takes off from B85 Schijndel in Spitfire IX RK853/SS in early 1945. It was in this aircraft whilst escorting Mitchells on 13 March that Sampson shot down a Bf 109 of 14./JG 27, flown by Unteroffizier Sepperl, to claim his final victory (*R W F Sampson*)

'In my Spitfire IXB, with my personal letters "SS" painted on the fuselage – a prerogative of a Wing Leader – I led Nos 329 and 74 Sqns on a sweep and armed recce into the Osnabrück area. We found the sky clear of enemy aircraft, but on the way back came across a train pulling 30 goods trucks. We severely damaged this, and also left some lorries in various stages of disrepair. We received plenty of flak when flying near Rheine airfield.'

Sampson's Wing moved to B85 Schijndel in early February, where Nos 340 and 341 Sqns later joined it. These units were both commanded by successful pilots, Cdt Oliver Massart and seven-victory ace Cdt Christian Martel (a *nom de guerre* for Pierre Montet).

## PUSH TO THE RHINE

Although poor weather conditions had resulted in a pause in the Allied advance into western Germany, preparations for a renewal of the offensive continued. The frontline largely lay along the German border, with the initial priority being to clear the Reichwald Forest of its formidable defence lines. The task was given to XXX Corps, and it launched Operation *Veritable* on 8 February behind a heavy artillery barrage and under an air umbrella that swept the ground ahead of the troops. The border town of Kleve fell the next day, despite fierce resistance.

On an armed reconnaissance over nearby Wesel on 8 February a patrol from No 442 Sqn came across five Ju 87 Stukas at low level that were attempting to support the German defenders. All of them were shot down, Flt Lt 'Chunky' Gordon despatching two in flames and sharing a third with Flt Lt Garry Doyle, who also shot down another. Flt Lt Bob Barker got the fifth for the first of his six claims, of which four were destroyed. The Spitfires were not deflected from their main task, however, as they continued with their mission, destroying three locomotives and ten lorries.

Sweeps behind the German lines attacking all manner of transport and infrastructure continued unabated. On Valentine's Day No 416 Sqn had a brief glimpse of the Luftwaffe when, near Münster, they spotted eight Me 262s escorting an Ar 234, but as the diary wistfully stated, 'they proved bashful and the enemy pilots opened up the burners and pulled away into cloud cover'. However, at Handorf some He 177 bombers were seen on the ground and several were shot up, with Jack Boyle destroying two of them. Ground attacks predominated, and during one on 22 February after Goch had been captured, No 442 Sqn's Sqn Ldr Milt

Jowsey was forced to bail out after his aircraft was hit by ricochets. Landing near Emmerich, he evaded capture for 40 days until his hideout was overrun by Allied troops.

Three days after losing its CO, the unit found the enemy in the air once again during a sweep to the Lingen-Wesel area, where No 442 Sqn engaged more than 40 Bf 109s and Fw 190s from II. and IV./JG 27. In a one-sided action seven were shot down, including a Bf 109 credited to Flt Lt 'Chunky' Gordon – he saw his rounds hit the fighter near the cockpit, and it crashed in flames. This was a very successful final Spitfire combat for No 442 Sqn, as soon after the unit returned to England to re-equip with Mustang IVs.

Having pushed through the Reichwald, Allied armies were on the banks of the Rhine by early March. However, the river proved to be a formidable natural barrier. German strong points and other defences were hit from the air, as Wg Cdr Sammy Sampson recalled;

'On 2 March I led all four squadrons against enemy mortar positions in the Hochwald Forest, again just a few hundred yards ahead of our troops. This time it was the Canadians who were being bogged down by the enemy mortars. I can say with some pride that we made no errors, such as strafing our own troops. Because of the strain on the wings when pulling out of an attack dive, the wings of our Spitfire XVIs were clipped.'

More wide-ranging sorties were also flown as preparations were made for crossing the river later in the month. On 1 March No 401 Sqn's solitary mission met with considerable success when the unit was bounced by enemy fighters. In the ensuing fight four Bf 109s were shot down. Sqn Ldr Bill Klersy wrote in his report;

'I called a break and positioned myself behind a Me 109. I opened fire at 500 yards, 30 degrees off, and observed strikes on the fuselage and drop tank, which burst into flames. I closed to 200 yards line astern and fired a two-second burst, which resulted in the enemy aircraft bursting into flames and spinning down into the deck, where it exploded. I got onto another Me 109 and fired a three-second burst from 300 yards at ten degrees off. There were strikes on the fuselage and wings, which finally resulted in the aircraft bursting into flames and spinning down to the deck, where it crashed.

'I then reformed my section and, looking out, I observed some FW 190s flying above us. I climbed toward them and positioned myself behind one. I opened fire at 400 yards 15 degrees off and didn't see any strikes. I went into line astern and fired a two-second burst, observing a strike on the canopy. The aircraft went through a thin layer of cloud in a shallow glide, which eventually steepened and it went straight into the deck and exploded.'

There was a great loss on 3 March when, in wet and stormy weather, Flt Lt Dick Audet attacked a train and was shot down by flak. This moving epitaph appeared in No 411 Sqn's record book;

'Modest and unassuming, he was just one of the boys, and a real credit to Canada and her RCAF. His daring and keenness led to his presumed death. He was a leader, respected and admired by all. Just one swell guy.'

The UK-based units also continued operations over the Continent, such as on 1 March when No 1 Sqn helped escort Lancasters attacking

From mid-January 1945 No 127 Wing was commanded by Battle of Britain ace Gp Capt Stan Turner, who flew a spitfire XVI TB300/PS-T. This aircraft carried the badge of No 421 Sqn on its nose (*via C H Thomas*)

an oil target near Kamen. Upon their return the fighters flew to Northolt for a special task. On 2 March the unit was tasked to provide escort to VIPs, including Prime Minister Winston Churchill, who were flying to the Continent, where the Spitfires landed to refuel. Then, on the 12th, when Bomber Command despatched more than 1000 heavy bombers to drop in excess of 5000 tons of ordnance on Dortmund, the escort was provided by Detling Wing Spitfires led by Wg Cdr Bobby Oxspring.

2nd TAF Spitfire units also regularly escorted the No 2 Group medium bombers. For example, on 13 March RAF Mitchells covered by Nos 74 and 340 Sqns from No 145 Wing were attacked east of Wesel by Bf 109s of 14./JG 27. Wg Cdr Sammy Sampson recalled the action, and his own final victory;

'After the Mitchells had dropped their bombs the first boxes opened their throttles and there was soon a gap of some three miles between the first two and the last box. I instructed Cdt Massart and his Yellow section to stay behind to guard them, whilst I and the other two sections stayed between the first and second box.

'Massart then called to say they were under attack by a dozen Me 109Gs. I approached and, horror of horrors, I heard Massart say that he had been badly hit and was going to have to bail out. As I closed in I was able to see the Me 109 still firing at Massart, and began to line up the Messerschmitt in my gyro gunsight at 800 yards. When I was at 600 yards the German pilot saw me, turning in my direction. I gave him a short burst of all my armament, having got him with both the "+" and the movable "dot" together. To my surprise I saw a strike on the front of his fighter, which seemed to knock him off balance because he then turned hard towards me, and my immediate reaction was once again, "You've had it boy". I easily out-turned him and got on his tail. I was still firing when the pilot bailed out, but I had the feeling that he was hit. Then the Me 109 disintegrated. By this time I was so close that my Spitfire was hit and slightly damaged by Hun debris, but it caused no serious problems.

'When I landed my rigger and fitter told me that there was blood on the leading edges of both wings, which tended to confirm that I had indeed hit the German pilot as he was attempting to get out.'

Massart was succeeded by the highly experienced six-victory ace Cdt 'Jaco' Andrieux.

Twenty-four hours earlier, in one of the few aerial combats fought at this time, Flt Lt Len Watt of No 401 Sqn spotted an Me 262 at 2500 ft just west of Wesel. Positioning himself astern of the jet, he fired two bursts that caused it to trail smoke and lose altitude. Its destruction was later confirmed, Watt having claimed the last jet destroyed by a Merlin Spitfire.

On 23 March, at the specific request of the Prime Minister, No 1 Sqn escorted his flight to Volkel. En route, some curious USAAF P-47 Thunderbolts appeared, and Sqn Ldr Cox weaved his Spitfires close to C-54B Skymaster EW999 (Churchill's personal transport) to fend them off. The following day saw the 21st Army Group begin crossing the Rhine from Emmerich, in the north, as part of Operation *Plunder*, whilst near Wesel an airborne assault, codenamed Operation *Varsity*, consolidated the crossing.

Covering the airborne operation was No 1 Sqn's final major operation with the Spitfire IX, its task being to patrol the route, and although there was plenty of flak, there was no aerial interference. 2nd TAF Spitfire squadrons were also heavily involved in escorting the transports and glider tugs. By the end of the day the link up between the 21st Army Group and the airborne troops had been achieved and a significant bridgehead established. The last major obstacle before the Reich had been breached. Sappers toiled to establish additional bridges under constant air cover, and despite fierce fighting Field Marshal Montgomery's 21st Army Group prepared to drive northeast to the Elbe and north into Holland, whilst the Ruhr basin was bypassed. Ahead of them, 2nd TAF tactical squadrons blasted a path and kept the skies clear.

## INTO GERMANY

As the Luftwaffe abandoned its western bases such as Rheine and retreated further east, so 2nd TAF wings moved into these recently vacated airfields. As ever, flak remained the most deadly foe, striking unexpectedly at low-flying aircraft. On 28 March Plt Off Mac Reeves, a successful pilot in No 411 Sqn, was shot down and killed attacking motorised transport near Dulmen, the same fate claiming V1 ace WO H C Cramm of the Dutch No 322 Sqn two days later whilst bombing an enemy HQ near Zutphen.

Having escorted Prime Minister Winston Churchill to Brussels on 2 March, Sqn Ldr Cox discovered that the tail wheel of his fighter (Spitfire IX MK644/JX-M) had jammed when landing back at Manston, causing the aircraft to cartwheel. Fortunately, the veteran pilot emerged from the wreck without serious injury (*D G S R Cox*)

The greatest Spitfire pilot of them all! In the centre of this group is Wg Cdr 'Johnnie' Johnson, who claimed all 41 of his victories flying the Supermarine fighter. He is surrounded by the No 127 Wing leadership cadre at Evere in January 1945. They are, from left to right, Sqn Ldr Danny Browne (OC No 421 Sqn, four destroyed and two damaged), Gp Capt W R 'Iron Bill' McBrien (CO No 127 Wing), Wg Cdr 'Johnnie' Johnson (No 127 Wing Wing Leader), Sqn Ldr Jim Collier (OC No 403 Sqn, two and one shared destroyed, one damaged and one probable) and Sqn Ldr E P 'Eep' Wood (previously OC No 403 Sqn, three and one shared destroyed, one probable and two damaged) (*P H T Green collection*)

The 28th also saw the CO of No 126 Wing, Battle of Britain ace Gp Capt Gordon McGregor, fly his final operational sortie – at 43 he was the oldest RCAF fighter pilot to see action during the war. One of his pilots in No 401 Sqn was Flt Lt John MacKay, who, near Coesfeld shortly after 1600 hrs, spotted a formation of six Bf 109s. He attacked the rear one and shot it down, and then when trying to rejoin the patrol spotted another Messerschmitt at ground level. Dropping onto it, he fired a single burst from his guns and saw the pilot bail out. The squadron diarist subsequently commented, 'Nice going, Johnny!'

A few minutes earlier Flt Lt John 'Webb' Harten of No 416 Sqn (in Spitfire XVI SM397/DN-V) shot down two Fw 190s near Emmerich to become No 416 Sqn's last ace. He had just commenced a patrol from Heerenberg east toward Sudlohn when a pair of Fw 190s approached him head-on, the German fighters being some 500 ft above him. Harten broke round to chase them, and as they flew in and out of cloud he gave the right hand aircraft two bursts that sent it spinning away in flames until it hit the ground. He then caught and shot down the second Focke-Wulf to reach ace status. Sadly, three weeks later, Harten also fell victim to flak when attacking a train, the Canadian crashing to his death near Kiebitzreihe.

On 30 March No 416 Sqn lost two of its aircraft shot down by USAAF Mustangs, although on this occasion the pilots fortunately survived – these types of attack were all too common in the final months of the war in Europe. The following day No 416 Sqn and No 127 Wing moved further north to B78 Eindhoven, and on 12 April the unit transferred onto German soil at B100 Goch. Forty-eight hours later No 416 Sqn moved again, this time to the former Luftwaffe airfield at B114 Diepholz. The unit's itinerant lifestyle was typical for 2nd TAF squadrons during this period.

The advance deep into the shrinking Reich continued apace, despite desperate opposition that inflicted heavy casualties on Allied soldiers and airmen alike. On 1 April, for example, no fewer than 13 Merlin-engined Spitfires were shot down by flak, with eight pilots killed. Luftwaffe fighters – often high-performance late model Bf 109G/Ks or Fw 190Ds – also appeared in strength on occasion, although aerial combat now rarely took place as 2nd TAF Spitfire units conducted a seemingly endless series of armed reconnaissance missions deep into Germany in search of enemy targets on the ground.

In early April the River Weser was crossed and the city of Hanover soon fell, whilst Allied fighter-bombers now concentrated their attacks on German airfields for several days. Spitfire XVIs of No 74 Sqn, for example, destroyed five fighters at Rotenburg on the 11th. Four days later 'Winston Churchill' also saw combat for the first time when presentation Spitfire XVI TB900/9N-F of No 127 Sqn was flown over Germany by WO Larry Hyland, the fighter bearing the Prime Minister's name beneath the cockpit.

Early the next morning (16 April) No 401 Sqn ace Flt Lt Johnny MacKay strafed Ludwigslust airfield in the face of heavy fire and damaged three Ar 234s.

Early that afternoon future ace Flg Off Denny Wilson (in RR201/DB-R) of No 411 Sqn had his first success when, near Grabow, he shot down a He 111. A little later Flt Lt Don Gordon was leading the unit looking for enemy motorised transport when they encountered an unusual opponent. Near Parchim he spotted a Ju 88/Fw 190 *Mistel* composite, but as he opened fire Gordon saw the combination separate, and he and his No 2 each shot down one component. The Ju 88 exploded, providing Gordon with his tenth victory, and only one with No 411 Sqn. He described this unusual kill as follows;

'After an hour of hunting for enemy motorised transport we crossed over Parchim aerodrome, where there was a Ju 88 starting to take off. When the pilot saw the Spitfires above him he quickly closed his throttles and slewed off the runway. We then orbited looking for any airborne enemy aircraft and spotted a Ju 88 with a FW 190 pick-a-back on it. I closed to 500 yards astern and opened fire. At the same time the FW 190 separated from the Ju 88. After my first burst large pieces flew off the Ju 88, and it soon caught fire and crashed. On hitting the ground it made a tremendous explosion. My No 3 [Flg Off Bazette] chased the FW 190 and shot it down in flames.'

Throughout April 1945 Spitfire XVI TB756/DN-H of No 416 Sqn was flown on armed reconnaissance missions by several aces, including Flt Lts John Harten and James Lindsay (*Canadian Forces*)

A clipped wing Spitfire XVI leads an unclipped fighter over B90 Kleine Brogel in the spring of 1945, both machines wearing the 2I codes of No 443 Sqn. The lead aircraft is TB476/2I-D, nicknamed *Ladykiller*, which was assigned to the CO, ace Sqn Ldr Art Sager (*Canadian Forces*)

Four *Mistels* from 6./KG 200 had been tasked with attacking bridges over the River Oder in Küstrin following the launching of a Soviet Red Army assault on the town earlier that same day. The aircraft downed by Gordon and Bazette was almost certainly one of these composites, and it is thought to have been the last *Mistel* to be shot down in combat by the Allied air forces – the identity of its pilot remains unknown.

Within a few days all of 2nd TAF's Spitfire squadrons were based on German soil, and on 19 April, during an early patrol over Hagenow airfield from its base at B116 Wunstorf, No 412 Sqn engaged some of the few remaining airworthy Luftwaffe fighters and shot four of them down. Flt Lt Don Pieri (flying Spitfire XVI NH471) destroyed one Fw 190 and shared a second with Flt Lt Lloyd Stewart to become an ace. Over the same airfield that afternoon Sqn Ldr Bill Klersy led No 401 Sqn in a strafing attack that was intercepted by Fw 190Ds from I./JG 26, and in a brief dogfight he shot down Fahnrich Gerhard von Plazer.

Klersy was in action again the following afternoon when No 401 Sqn spotted aircraft taking off from a grass strip near Schwerin. Braving the airfield defences, the RCAF pilots shot down 11 Bf 109s. Among the successful pilots was Johnny MacKay, who claimed his final victory of the war. He subsequently increased his score in 1953 while flying F-86s with the USAF during the Korean War. Bill Klersy (flying Spitfire IX PL344/YO-H) was credited with one shot down and a second shared with Flt Lt Leroy Woods. On a later patrol that same day No 401 Sqn enjoyed yet more success when, over Hagenow airfield, seven Fw 190s were claimed. Bill Klersy (again in PL344/YO-H) shot down two to register his final claims in the air, whilst Flg Off Gregory 'Cam' Cameron in shooting down one of the Focke-Wulfs took his score to five, and thus become No 401 Sqn's last ace. Ten days later, on 1 May, he was shot down by flak, although he evaded capture and returned to his unit on the 2nd.

During the late afternoon of 21 April, No 403 Sqn's CO, Sqn Ldr Hank Zary, flying his Spitfire XVI TB752/KH-Z, shot down a Bf 109 near Schnackenburg to also become a Spitfire ace. His aircraft had only been delivered to the squadron two days earlier, and on the 25th, when flown by Flg Off Leslie, it destroyed another enemy aircraft, which was thought to have been a Focke-Wulf Fw 189 tactical reconnaissance aircraft. Then on 1 May, with Flg Off Young at the controls, it claimed its third successful combat – an Fw 190. TB752 survived the war and is now on display at the Spitfire Memorial Museum at Manston Airport in Kent. Four days after becoming an ace, during a strafing attack on Schwerin airfield, Zary damaged an Me 262 and a Ju 88 on the ground for his final claims. Sadly, soon after the war Hank Zary contracted pleurisy and died in an Ottawa hospital in February 1946.

On 27 April, despite fierce opposition, the port city of Bremen fell, and further to the west Canadian troops reached the Ems Estuary. Two days later the River Elbe was crossed by elements of the 2nd Army with relative ease. 29 April also saw one of the leading Canadian aces of World War 2 return to action as leader of No 127 Wing. Wg Cdr J F 'Eddie' Edwards was flying his personal Spitfire XVI TD147/JFE at the time, his post-war biography describing his first mission as follows;

'On 29 April he flew two missions. The first was uneventful and the second was a patrol in an area where the Germans had been dive-bombing. He and his wingman spotted an Fw 190 using heavy cumulus as cover to attack Allied ground troops and headed it off. They registered hits on the aircraft, but it escaped into cloud. Shortly thereafter, another aircraft popped out of a cloud. This time it was a brand new, and deadly, Messerschmitt 262 jet. As he was travelling very fast the Spitfires had no chance to catch him, so Eddie and his wingman fired at long range and saw hits on the fuselage. The jet kept going and disappeared into a cloud. The next day he got shots off at another 262, but it climbed away from them and easily escaped.'

The desperate attempts by the Luftwaffe to support the crumbling fronts to both east and west saw 2nd TAF units continue to reap a rich harvest. Nine aircraft of No 412 Sqn led by the CO flew an armed reconnaissance in the Hamburg area on the evening of 30 April. Flt Lt Don Pieri had taken off as a spare, and at around 1930 hrs just as he was about to return home he spotted an Fw 190. His combat report vividly described the action;

'Just about 15 miles east of Hamburg I saw four FW 190s heading east on the deck as I was heading north. They turned and flew northwest, while I gave chase. When I got in range, two broke starboard on the deck and two broke port up into cloud. I got a good shot of three seconds from about 20-30 degrees at one on the deck from about 400 yards. I then had to break off combat and break port into the two FW 190s that had gone into cloud. They both overshot me, and I got a squirt at one. Just before I opened fire on the second FW 190, I saw one of the other two explode as it hit the deck. I took a quick squirt at the second FW 190 and then broke up into cloud.'

The main patrol was just to the northeast of the Elbe bridgehead at Lauenburg ten minutes later when they spotted more fighters. In the subsequent fight Flt Lt Bob Barker shot one down and damaged a second to frustratingly leave his total at four destroyed and two damaged, and so he narrowly missed becoming an ace. Flt Lt Lloyd Stewart claimed another to register his fifth combat claim, three of which were destroyed. However, the honours went to their CO, Sqn Ldr Maurice Boyd, who, at the controls of Spitfire IX PV234, shot down two Bf 109s and damaged a third to thus become the last pilot of the Northwest Europe campaign to become an ace whilst flying a Merlin-engined Spitfire.

# SURRENDER

s May began 2nd TAF fighters continued to roam virtually unmolested over what little remained of the Reich, and many successful pilots made their final claims. Late in the afternoon of the 1st, No 127 Wing Wing Leader, nine-victory ace Wg Cdr Geoff Northcott (flying his personally-marked Spitfire IX PV229 JEFF), was over Schwerin airfield when he damaged an Fw 190. Shortly thereafter, during an evening patrol, No 401 Sqn CO Sqn Ldr Bill Klersy had his final aerial combat when, over Lübeck airfield, he also damaged an Fw 190. However, his squadronmate Flt Lt 'Cam' Cameron, who had become an ace just ten days earlier, was shot down by flak over Schwerin. Although he was badly burned bailing out of his blazing Spitfire, Cameron managed to escape and make his way back to Allied lines.

With the war entering its final week, Field Marshal Montgomery's forces continued their thrust deep into Northwest Germany towards the Baltic coast, capturing the port of Lübeck on 2 May. This proved to be as far east as the western Allies got.

That morning Spitfires of No 411 Sqn caught a pair of Bf 109s from 1./NAGr 3 near Lübeck, and the aircraft flown by Oberleutnant Burghard was shot down by Flt Lt Denny Wilson for his second victory. Wilson was to achieve acedom flying for the Israelis in 1948 when he shot down three Egyptian fighters to become the last pilot to achieve this distinction in the Spitfire. Later, at around 1600 hrs, pilots from No 443 Sqn shot down a Fieseler Fi 156 Storch and a He 111. Ten minutes later another section led by Flt Lt Hartland Finley downed a Ju 88 near Bad Segeberg. However, return fire from Finley's fifth claim, four of which were destroyed, set his aircraft on fire and he had to bail out from just 200 ft.

**Flt Lt Hartland Finley of No 443 Sqn sits on the cockpit edge of Spitfire XVI SM204/2I-J, which he was flying on the afternoon of 2 May when he shared in the destruction of a Ju 88 near Bad Segeberg. He was in turn hit by defensive fire from the bomber and forced to bail out at just 200 ft (*via Larry Milberry*)**

The next day the shattered city of Hamburg fell, and the 2nd Army made contact with the Soviet Red Army at Grabow.

Although the Luftwaffe was now largely absent flak remained an ever-present danger, and south of Kiel during the morning of the 3rd No 411 Sqn's Flt Lt Stan McClarty radioed that he had been hit in the leg but then dived into the ground and was killed. He had made seven aerial claims, including four destroyed. Then, just before midday, when a section from No 412 Sqn was carrying out a strafing attack again near Kiel, Flt Lt Don Pieri's Spitfire IX was hit by ricochets. Although he successfully bailed out, he was captured by the Hitler Youth and subsequently murdered. Don Pieri, whose body was never found, was the last ace to fall in a Merlin-engined Spitfire in Europe. In a tragic irony, the squadron flew its final war sorties the following day.

Several hours after this tragedy No 401 Sqn saw its last action with Merlin-engined Spitfires. Whilst covering the British and Canadian entry into Hamburg, pilots from the unit spotted a large number of aircraft on the ground in various stages of camouflage at Schönberg airfield. Diving down, they destroyed two He 111s, a solitary Ju 87 and no fewer than 12 Ju 52/3m transports. As the diarist commented, 'Not bad for a short day's work!' One of the He 111s was credited to Sqn Ldr Bill Klersy in what proved to be his final action.

Early on the evening of 3 May, when flying with No 443 Sqn, Wg Cdr Eddie Edwards, Wing Leader of No 127 Wing, shared in the destruction of a Ju 88 spotted flying over Eckerndorfer Bay to the west of the small Baltic port of Kappeln to take his total to 18. Significantly, No 443 Sqn's final 'scalp' was also the last enemy aircraft destroyed by an ace in a Merlin-engined Spitfire during the campaign in Northwest Europe. Edwards' biography outlined the event as follows;

'Eddie's 373rd, and last, combat sortie ended in the same way as his first had – with the downing of an enemy aircraft. He was leading No 443 Sqn on an armed recce north of Kiel when a Ju 88 was spotted. One flight dove on the aircraft and peppered it with cannon and machine gun fire, but it refused to go down. Eddie brought his flight down behind the

Shortly before midday on 3 May seven-victory ace Flt Lt Don Pieri of No 412 Sqn took off from B116 Wunstorf in this aircraft, Spitfire IX MK827. A short while later, when carrying out a strafing run near Kiel, a ricochet struck the fighter. Forced to bail out, Pieri was immediately captured and subsequently murdered by members of the Hitler Youth. He was the last ace to be killed flying a Merlin-engined Spitfire (*Canadian Forces*)

Wg Cdr Eddie Edwards was one of the leading RCAF aces of World War 2, and he returned to lead No 127 Wing in April 1945. Flying his personal Spitfire XVI TD147/JF-E, he damaged an Fw 190 and an Me 262 on the 29th. Edwards was at its controls again on 3 May when he helped bring down a Ju 88 that proved to be the last kill claimed by an ace in a Merlin-engined Spitfire. It took Edwards' victory tally to 18 (*J F Edwards*)

aeroplane and fired a long burst at it. With both engines on fire the aeroplane crashed. This was the last wartime victory of No 127 Wing.'

Forty minutes later Plt Off Larry Spurr and Flg Off Rex Tapley of No 416 Sqn shot down a Do 217 over Swarzenbeck to the east of Hamburg to claim the unit's 75th victory. Coincidentally, its first, in 1942, had also been a Do 217! Early the following morning (4 May) an armed reconnaissance from No 411 Sqn took off at 0540 hrs for the Kiel area, and an hour later, near Flensburg, it found an He 111 that Flt Lt D F Campbell and Flg Off T L O'Brien shot down, as the latter described in his combat report;

With the war just over, the Norwegian ace and CO of No 332 Sqn, Maj Ola Aanjesen, completes his final sortie in Spitfire IX NH316/AH-O prior to flying back to his homeland (*via Nils Mathisrud*)

Flying Spitfire IX MK686/DB-L on 4 May, Flt Lt T L O'Brien helped shoot down a He 111 that was the last victim of a Merlin-engined Spitfire in Europe. On Christmas Day 1944 Flt Lt Johnny Boyle had used the same Spitfire to shot down an Me 262 (*PAC*)

Personnel of No 411 Sqn pose for the camera in April 1945 at B88 Heesch. In the back row, from left to right, are Flg Off T E Vance, Plt Off D B Young, Flg Offs J V McCabe, J T Olson, B A McPhail and J L St John, Sqn Ldr J N Newell (sat on the propeller hub), Flg Off M R Macklem, Flt Lt A Ustenov, Flg Offs C D W Wilson and G N Smith, Flt Lt W A Reid and Plt Off J O A Watt. In the front row, from left to right, are Flg Offs H Martensen, T L O'Brien and C A E Ellement, Flt Lts J M McConnell and D J Bazett, Flg Off J A Doran, Flt Lt D C Gordon, Flg Off G R Panchuk (Intelligence Officer), Flt Lts J J Boyle, W T Gill, M F Doyle and A A W Orr and Flg Offs M G Graham, J F Shiriff and W G Pryde (*Public Archives of Canada PMR 78-342*)

'I went down with my No 1 to attack a train north of Flensburg. At 600 ft Flt Lt Campbell sighted a He 111 flying south and then I sighted it, and we attacked from dead astern. Flt Lt Campbell and I opened fire at about 250-300 yards, and strikes were seen on the starboard engine and wing. The engine poured smoke and pieces were observed falling off. Then the aircraft crashed into a field. No one got out.'

This was No 411 Sqn's last aerial victory, and also the last for No 126 Wing, which finished the war as the top-scoring Spitfire Wing in 2nd TAF.

Thus, in the grey, overcast, skies of Northwest Germany fell the last enemy aircraft to be claimed by a Merlin-engined Spitfire in Europe – almost five-and-a-half years after the first one had been destroyed. Three days later the Germans unconditionally surrendered.

# APPENDICES

## Spitfire Aces of Northwest Europe 1944-45

| Name | Service | Unit/s | 2nd TAF Claims | Total Claims | Theatre/s |
|---|---|---|---|---|---|
| Laubman D C | RCAF | 412 | 14+2sh/-/3 | 14+2sh/-/3 | UK, Eur |
| Klersy W T | RCAF | 401 | 14+1sh/-/3 | 14+1sh/-/3 | UK, Eur |
| Johnson J E | RAF | 144 Wg, 127 Wg | 13/-/1 | 34+7sh/3+2sh/10+3sh | UK, Eur |
| MacKay J | RCAF | 401 | 10+2sh/-/3+1sh | 11+2sh/-/3+1sh | Eur |
| Audet R J | RCAF | 411 | 10+1sh/-/1 | 10+1sh /-/1 | Eur |
| Banks W J | RCAF | 412 | 9/3/1 | 9/3/1 | Eur |
| Trainor H C | RCAF | 411, 401 | 8+1sh/1/- | 8+1sh/1/- | UK, Eur |
| Page A G | RAF | 132, 125 Wg | 6+3sh/-/3 | 10+5sh/-/3 | UK, Eur |
| Johnson G W | RCAF | 411, 401 | 8/-/4 | 8/-/4 | UK, Eur |
| Jamieson D R C | RCAF | 412 | 8/-/1 | 8/-/1 | Eur |
| McLeod H W | RCAF | 443 | 8/-/- | 21/3/12 +1sh | UK, Eur |
| Smith R I A | RCAF | 401, 412 | 7+1sh/-/- | 13+1sh/1sh/1 | Eur |
| Pieri D M | RCAF | 442, 412 | 5+2sh/-/2 | 5+2sh/-/2 | UK, Eur |
| Gordon D C | RCAF | 442, 411 | 5+2sh/-/- | 9+2sh/5/5 | Eur |
| Lindsay J D | RCAF | 403, 416 | 6/-/6 | 8+1sh/-/8 | UK, Eur |
| Le Roux J J | RAF | 602 | 6/-/2 | 18/2/8 | Eur |
| Mitchner J D | RCAF | 402, 421, 416 | 6/-/- | 10+1sh/1+2sh/3 | UK, Eur |
| Kimball D H | RCAF | 441 | 6/-/- | 6/-/- | UK, Eur |
| Hayward R K | RCAF | 401, 411 | 5+1sh/-/5+1sh | 5+1sh/1sh/5+1sh | UK |
| Boyle J J | RCAF | 411 | 5+1sh/-/1 | 5+1sh/-/1 | Eur |
| Mott G E | RCAF | 441 | 5+1sh/-/- | 5+1sh/-/- | UK |
| Lapp E G | RCAF | 411 | 4+2sh/-/1 | 4+2sh/-/1 | Eur |
| Murray F T | RCAF | 412, 401 | 5/1/2+1sh | 5/1/2+1sh | Eur |
| Cameron G D A T | RCAF | 401 | 5/1/2 | 5/1/3 | Eur |
| Johnson P G | RCAF | 421 | 5/1/- | 5/1/2 | UK |
| Bouskill R R | RCAF | 401 | 5/-/3 | 5/-/3 | Eur |
| Zary P M | RCAF | 421, 403 | 5/-/2 | 5/-/2 | UK, Eur |
| Charron P M | RCAF | 412 | 5/-/1 | 7/-/2 | Eur |
| Graham M G | RCAF | 411 | 5/-/- | 5/-/- | Eur |
| Boyd M D | RCAF | 412 | 4+1sh/-/2 | 4+1sh/-/2 | UK, Eur |
| Gordon M J | RCAF | 403, 421 | 4+1sh/-/1 | 4+1sh/-/1 | UK, Eur |
| Gran M Y | Nor | 331 | 4+1sh/-/1 | 8+2sh/2/5+1sh | UK, Eur |
| Robertson G D | RCAF | 421, 411 | 4+1sh/-/1 | 4+1sh/1/4+1sh | UK, Eur |
| Harling D W A | RCAF | 416 | 4+1sh/-/1 | 4+1sh/-/1 | Eur |
| Lake R G | RCAF | 441 | 4+1sh/-/1 | 4+1sh/-/1 | UK, Eur |
| Ockenden G F | RCAF | 443 | 4+1sh/-/1 | 4+1sh /-/1 | UK, Eur |
| Davenport R M | RCAF | 401 | 4+1sh/-/1 | 4+1sh/-/1 | Eur |
| Reeves M* | RCAF | 403 | 4/-/1 | 4/-/1 | Eur |

# Aces with some Spitfire claims in Northwest Europe 1944-45

| Name | Service | Unit/s | 2nd TAF Claims | Total Claims | Theatre/s |
|---|---|---|---|---|---|
| Aanjesen O G | Nor | 332, 331 | 3/-/-+1 V1 | 5+1sh/1/1+4sh+1 V1 | UK, Eur |
| Andrieux J | Fr | 341 | 3/-/- | 6/4/2 | UK |
| Ayerst P V | RAF | 124 | 1sh/-/- | 3+2sh/1/3 | UK |
| Berg R A | Nor | 132 Wg | 3/-/- | 6/2/3+3sh | UK, Eur |
| Bird-Wilson H A C | RAF, | Harrowbeer Wg, 122 Wg | 1/-/- | 3+6sh/3/3 | UK |
| Birksted K | Dan | 132 Wg | 1/-/- | 10+1sh/-/5 | UK |
| Bjornstad B | Nor | 80 | 1sh/-/- | 5+1sh/-/3+2sh | UK |
| Boudier M | Fr | 341 | 1/-/- | 8/-/7 | UK, Eur |
| Brannagan T A | RCAF | 403, 441 | 3+1sh/-/1 | 3+2sh/-/1 | UK, Eur |
| Brothers P M | RAF | Exeter Wg, Culmhead Wg | 1/-/- | 16/1/3 | UK |
| Cameron L M | RCAF | 401 | 3/-/1 | 6/-/2 | UK |
| Campbell F | RAF | 132 | 2/-/2 | 5?/2/6+1sh | UK, Eur |
| Charney K L | RAF | 602, 132 | 3/1/2 | 6/4/7 | UK, Eur |
| Checketts J M | RNZAF | 1, 142 Wg | 2/-/1 | 14/3/8+2 V1 | UK, Eur |
| Christie W | Nor | 332 | 1+1sh/-/1 | 9+1sh/1/4+1sh | UK |
| Clostermann P H | Fr | 602 | 4/3/2 | 11(+5 more?)/2/9 | UK |
| Conrad W A G | RCAF | 421 | -/-/2 | 5+3sh/3/10+2sh | Eur |
| Cox D G S R | RAF | 504, 222, 1 | -/-/1 | 7+1sh/6/5 | UK |
| Crawford H A* | RCAF | 411 | 2/-/- | 2+1sh/-/- | Eur |
| Crawford-Compton W V | RAF | 145 Wg | 4/-/- | 21+1sh/3+1sh/13 | UK, Eur |
| Dogger R | Nor | 331 | 4/-/- | 6/-/1 | UK, Eur |
| Douglas W A | RAF | 611, Coltishall Wg | 2/-/- | 6/2+1sh/7 | UK |
| Dover D H | RCAF | 442, 412 | 2+1sh/-/3 | 3+2sh/-/3 | UK, Eur |
| Dowding H J | RCAF | 442 | 2/-/1 | 5+3sh/-/3 | UK |
| Edwards J F | RCAF | 274, 127 Wg | 1sh/-/2 | 15+3sh/8+1sh/13 | Eur |
| Everard H J | RCAF | 401 | 2+1sh/1/- | 5+1sh/3/3 | Eur |
| Fairbanks D C | RCAF | 501 | 1/-/1 | 12+1sh/-/3 | UK |
| Giddings K C M | RAF | 118 | 1sh/-/- | 4+1sh/1/5 | Eur |
| Gouby R G | Fr | 165, 611 | 1/-/- | 9/1/3 | UK |
| Graham M | RAF | 132 | 2/-/- | 4+2sh/1/3 | UK, Eur |
| Grant R J C | RNZAF | 122 Wg | 1sh/-/- | 7+1sh/1/- | UK |
| Grundt-Spang H G E | Nor | 331 | 4/-/1 | 10+1sh/2/2+1sh | Eur |
| Hall D I | RCAF | 400, 414 | 3/-/- | 7/-/2 | Eur |
| Harries R H | RAF | 135 Wg | 1/-/1 | 15+3sh/2/5+1sh+1 V1 | UK, Eur |
| Harrison G A | RAF | 616 | 1/-/- | 3+2sh/+1sh/- | UK |
| Harten J W E | RCAF | 416 | 2/-/- | 3+2sh/-/- | Eur |
| Hibbert W J | RAF | 124 | 1sh/-/- | 4+2sh/-/2 | UK |
| Hill G U | RCAF | 441 | 1sh/-/- | 10+8sh/3/10 | UK |
| Houlton J A | RNZAF | 485 | 3+1sh/-/1 | 5+2sh/-/4 | UK, Eur |
| Hughes J C | RCAF | 401 | 2/-/- | 2+3sh/-/+1sh | Eur |
| Husband D F | RCAF | 401 | 4/-/1 | 5+1sh/-/3 | Eur |

| Name | Service | Unit/s | 2nd TAF Claims | Total Claims | Theatre/s |
|------|---------|--------|----------------|--------------|-----------|
| Johnston H A S | RAF | 165, 66 | 1/-/- | 5+1sh/5/2+1sh | UK |
| Jörstad N K | Nor | 331 | 2+1sh/-/- | 6+1sh/2/4+1sh | UK, Eur |
| Jowsey M E | RCAF | 442 | 1/1/- | 5/1/3 | Eur |
| Keefer G C | RCAF | 412, 126 Wg | 4/-/- | 12/2/9 | UK, Eur |
| Kennedy I F | RCAF | 401 | 2/-/- | 10+5sh/1/- | UK |
| Kingaby D E | RAF | HQ FC (att 501) | 1/-/- | 21+2sh/6/1 | UK |
| Lofts K T | RAF | 66 | -/-/1 | 3+4sh/1+1sh/6+1sh | UK |
| Mackenzie A R | RCAF | 421, 403 | 4/-/1 | 8+1sh/-/1 | UK |
| McElroy J F | RCAF | 421, 416 | 3+1sh/-/1 | 13+3sh/1+1sh/12 | UK, Eur |
| Moore L A | RCAF | 402, 441 | 2+2sh/-/- | 3+3sh/1/1+1sh | UK |
| Neil J W | RCAF | 441, 421 | 2/1/- | 5/3/6 | Eur |
| Niven J B | RAF | 485 | -/-/1 | 2+3sh/3/5 | UK |
| Noonan D E | RCAF | 416 | 3+1sh/-/- | 4+3sh/-/- | UK, Eur |
| Northcott G W | RCAF | 402, 126 Wg | -/-/1 | 8+1sh/1/7+1sh | UK, Eur |
| Plagis J A | Rhod | 64, 126 | 3/-/1 | 15+2sh/2+2sh/6+1sh | UK, Eur |
| Robillard J G L | RCAF | 411, 442, 443 | 3/-/- | 7/-/1 | UK, Eur |
| Russel B D | RCAF | 127 Wg, 442, 126 Wg | 1sh/-/1 | 2+5sh/2/4 | UK, Eur |
| Sager A H | RCAF | 416, 443 | 2/-/1 | 4+2sh/1/5+1sh | Eur |
| Sampson R W F* | RAF | 131, 127, 145 Wg | 2/-/- | 4/1/5 | Eur |
| Sheppard J E | RCAF | 401, 412 | 4/-/- | 5/-/- | UK, Eur |
| Smit O | Czech | 310 | 2+1sh/-/- | 8+2sh/2/3+3 V1 | UK |
| Smith D H | RAAF | 453 | 1/1/2 | 5+1sh/2/2 | UK |
| Thorne J N | RAF | 64, 504 | 1sh/-/- | 4+2sh/1sh/4 | UK |
| Troke G W | RCAF | 443 | 2+1sh/-/1 | 5+3sh/1/5 | UK, Eur |
| Walmsley H E | RAF | 132 | 1/-/- | 11+1sh/1/4 | UK |
| Wells E P | RAF | Tangmere, Detling and West Malling Wgs | -/-/+1 on gnd | 12/4/6+1sh | UK |
| Wilson C D W | RCAF | 411 | 2/-/1 | 5/-/1 | Eur |
| Wilson F A W J | RAF | 402, 441, 443 | 1/1/2 | 8+1sh/2/5 | UK, Eur |
| Wonnacott G | RCAF | 414 | 2/-/- | 4+2sh/-/- | Eur |
| Yule R D | RAF | 125 Airfield | 1/-/1 | 3+5sh/2+1sh/1+3sh | UK |

**Theatre Key**
**UK** – United Kingdom pre-D-Day and escort operations
**Eur** – France and Germany post-D-Day

* – Pilots that appear in the Grub Street volumes *Aces High*, *Those Other Eagles* or *Stars & Bars* and who have less than five victories, but where there is uncertainty as to their actual total

# COLOUR PLATES

## 1

### Spitfire IX MH883/VZ-B of Flt Lt G F Beurling, No 412 Sqn RCAF, Hutton Cranswick and Biggin Hill, January-February 1944

The brilliant but enigmatic Canadian George Beurling achieved incredible success in the bitter fighting over Malta during 1942. In late 1943 he returned to action with the RCAF from Britain, initially with No 403 Sqn and then with No 412. With the latter unit his usual mount was MH883, in which he claimed an Fw 190 during a sweep on 30 December 1943. This was Beurling's 32nd, and last, victory. He continued to fly this aircraft into 1944, by which time his groundcrew had adorned it with his impressive victory tally – it was photographed so marked on 20 February, shortly before Beurling returned to Canada. Interestingly, although many of his Malta victims were Italian, all are recorded with a swastika. Having survived World War 2, MH883 was sold to the Turkish Air Force post-war.

## 2

### Spitfire IX MK426/SK-D of Flt Lt T Spencer, No 165 Sqn, Predannack, 25 April 1944

No 165 Sqn was based in the southwest of England as part of No 10 Group during the months before D-Day. Among its pilots were several who would gain success during the campaign against the V1 later in the summer. One such individual was Flt Lt Terry Spencer, who claimed eight V1s and subsequently commanded No 350 (Belgian) Sqn, equipped with Spitfire XIVs in the closing weeks of the war. At 1045 hrs on 25 April 1944 he was scrambled in MK426 after an unidentified 'plot', but when he closed on the 'intruder' it turned out to be an Anson. MK426 was also regularly flown by another V1 ace, Flg Off 'Ac' Lawson, on standing patrols off the south coast in the weeks before D-Day. Post-war, MK426 was transferred to the Danish Air Force.

## 3

### Spitfire VII MD120/NX-O of Sqn Ldr J J O'Meara, No 131 Sqn, Culmhead, March-June 1944

No 131 Sqn was affiliated with the County of Kent, and some of its Spitfire VIIs that were finished in high-altitude colours and fitted with extended wingtips were suitably adorned. One such aircraft was MD120/NX-O, christened *Spirit of Kent*. The personal mount of the CO, Sqn Ldr 'Orange' O'Meara, who had 12 victories to his name, MD120 was flown by the ace on No 131 Sqn's first operation with the Spitfire VII – a 'Ramrod' escorting Mosquitoes sent to attack a V1 site near Neufchatel – on 18 March. O'Meara continued to fly this aircraft until he left the squadron in late May. It was then taken over by his successor, Sqn Ldr Ian MacDougal, who flew it on a sweep on the evening of D-Day. MD120 was later transferred to No 154 Sqn for long-range escort work, and it was scrapped in March 1945.

## 4

### Spitfire VB AB509/JMC of Wg Cdr J M Checketts, No 142 Wing, Friston, May-June 1944

When appointed as the Wing Leader of No 142 Wing in May 1944, 12-victory ace Wg Cdr Johnny Checketts adopted Spitfire VB AB509 as his personal mount. Wearing his initials in the conventional style (as well as a command pennant and RCAF and Polish unit emblems), the fighter was regularly flown by Checketts. When AEAF stripes were added just before the Normandy invasion the codes were overpainted, although they were hastily scrawled back on in chalk! On D-Day Checketts flew AB509 four times, and on the 8th he was at its controls when he led No 501 Sqn on a patrol over the beachhead. As the RAF fighters flew over the mouth of the River Orne they encountered six Bf 109s, one of which Checketts damaged, and others claimed two destroyed and a probable. Checketts remained in the RNZAF post-war, whilst AB509 ended its days with No 53 Operational Training Unit (OTU).

## 5

### Spitfire VII EN509/ON-G of Flt Lt W J Hibbert, No 124 Sqn, Bradwell Bay, 31 May 1944

Throughout May 1944 the high-flying Spitfire VIIs of No 124 Sqn regularly patrolled the Thames Estuary, and during that period this aircraft was flown by a number of aces. Early in the month Flt Lt Gareth Nowell flew EN509, whilst on the 12th Flt Lt Peter Ayerst undertook a patrol in it, as did Flt Lt Jesse Hibbert during the evening of 31 May. The latter two pilots claimed one of No 124 Sqn's few victories after D-Day when, on the evening of 12 June, they shot down a high-flying Bf 109 over the Channel. His share in this success took Ayerst to acedom. With Flt Sgt Patterson at the controls, EN509/ON-G participated in No 124's final Spitfire VII operation – a 'Rodeo' escorting Halifaxes and Lancasters to attack tactical targets near Caen – on 18 July.

## 6

### Spitfire VII MD182/YQ-E of Flt Lt G A Harrison, No 616 'South Yorkshire' Sqn, Culmhead, 4 June 1944

On 27 May recently arrived flight commander Flt Lt Geoffrey Harrison, who had gained two and two shared victories in North Africa, flew his first operational sortie with No 616 Sqn – a patrol over Portland naval base. Two days earlier, Spitfire VII MD182 had been issued to the unit, and Harrison flew it twice on 4 June – on a dawn patrol and during a mid morning (1000-1130 hrs) mission – as No 616 Sqn protected shipping crammed into the ports of southern England prior to the imminent invasion of France. During a sweep over Laval on 12 June the extended wingtip of Harrison's Spitfire VII (MD121) took the tail off a Bf 109, which crashed, giving him his fifth victory. However, moments later, Harrison's own aircraft became uncontrollable and crashed before he could bail out. MD182 survived the war and was expended as a target on the Shoeburyness live firing range in 1948.

## 7

### Spitfire IX MK379/FU-? of Sqn Ldr D H Smith, No 453 Sqn RAAF, Ford, June 1944

When Sqn Ldr Don Smith, who had become an ace in 1943, took command of No 453 Sqn in late April 1944 he had a '?' painted in place of an individual aircraft letter on his personal Spitfire IX. He flew MK379 throughout May on bomber escort missions, such as covering a Boston raid on Cambrai on the

7th and USAAF B-26s targeting Berck the following day. Smith flew his first patrol on D-Day in another aircraft, but he was flying MK379 on beachhead patrols during the afternoon and evening, and he regularly used it on further missions over France during the next few weeks. Indeed, on a sortie during the evening of 16 June a patrol of No 453 Sqn Spitfires ran into 12 Bf 109s over Caen, one of which Don Smith damaged in the ensuing dogfight. MK379 survived the war and was struck off charge in 1946.

# 8

**Spitfire IX ML407/OU-V of Flg Off J A Houlton, No 485 Sqn RNZAF, Selsey, Coolham, Funtington and Tangmere, May-August 1944**

ML407 was the regular aircraft of Flg Off Johnny Houlton, but it had gone unserviceable on D-Day, so for his first sorties he flew MK950, in which he was credited with the first aircraft shot down after the invasion. However, he was flying ML407 two days later when he shot down a Bf 109 near Caen to claim his fifth victory. He was also in ML407 when, on a dawn patrol on 12 June, he shot down another Bf 109 that was also No 485 Sqn's final victory of the war, although he was also to claim a damaged in the fighter later in the month. The aircraft is shown as it appeared during late August, complete with a small pink elephant motif beneath the cockpit. After the war Houlton remained in the RNZAF. Following lengthy service ML407 also survived to be converted into a two-seater for the Irish Army Air Corps. Restored to airworthiness in the early 1980s, it has been owned by the Grace family in England for more than three decades.

# 9

**Spitfire IX MK392/JE-J of Wg Cdr J E Johnson, No 144 Wing, Ford and B3 St Croix-sur-Mer, June-July 1944**

The most successful RAF pilot in the Northwest Europe campaign, Wg Cdr 'Johnnie' Johnson was Wing Leader of the RCAF's No 144 Wing in the spring of 1944, with MK392 as his personal aircraft. Between March and September, by which time the fighter had moved with him to No 127 Wing, he had claimed 12 victories whilst flying it. The last came during the fighting around Arnhem on 27 September, when he shot down a Bf 109 near Rees. This was also his final victory, taking his tally to 34 and 7 shared destroyed. Post-war Johnson had a successful career in the RAF, eventually attaining the rank of Air Vice-Marshal, but MK392 was burnt out following a crash in April 1945 whilst serving with No 401 Sqn.

# 10

**Spitfire VB BM635/2Y-H of Cdt 'Bernard' (J M Accart), No 345 (French) Sqn, Shoreham, 17 June 1944**

'Bernard' was the *nom de guerre* adopted by the CO of No 345 Sqn, Cdt Jean Accart. A successful ace from the Battle of France, he had claimed 12 victories before being wounded. In January 1944 Accart had formed No 345 Sqn in Ayr following its move to the UK from French North Africa, and he led it on operations in the weeks before the invasion. BM635 was the usual mount of the flight commander, Cne Gaston Guizard, but at dawn on 17 June Jean Accart flew it on a low cover patrol over *Omaha* beach, where, despite good visibility, complete cloud cover meant that the patrol was uneventful. Like many Free French aircraft, BM635 wears a Cross of Lorraine badge beneath its cockpit. This aircraft ended its service career with No 61 OTU.

# 11

**Spitfire IX MJ586/LO-D of Sous-Lt P H Clostermann, No 602 'City of Glasgow' Sqn, B11 Longues, France, 28-29 June 1944**

Free French ace Pierre Clostermann joined No 602 Sqn in 1943 and flew with the unit throughout the Normandy invasion, reaching acedom on 26 June. He was assigned MJ586 for much of this time, the aircraft featuring No 602 Sqn's rampant lion badge on its nose and his scoreboard beneath the cockpit. On the 28th Clostermann was involved in a dogfight with some Fw 190s and the following day he engaged more Focke-Wulfs near Rouen, one of which he shot down to claim his sixth victory. Clostermann was in action in MJ586 again the next day when, near Vire, he again fought with Fw 190s, one of which he claimed as a 'probable'. He left No 602 Sqn soon afterwards, but returned to action flying Tempest Vs in early 1945, claiming additional victories. MJ586 also had a long career until it was written off following a crash-landing whilst serving with No 165 Sqn in 1946.

# 12

**Spitfire IX MK777/Y2-Z of Flt Lt H J Dowding, No 442 Sqn RCAF, B3 St Croix-sur-Mer, France, 27-28 June 1944**

In March 1944 Harry Dowding, who had become an ace during 1943, joined the newly arrived No 442 Sqn as a flight commander, and he was in action with the unit throughout the spring and summer. He flew MK777 regularly, and was at its controls over Normandy, near Lisieux, at just after midday on 27 June when No 442 Sqn became embroiled in a dogfight with Bf 109s, two of which fell to Dowding's fire for him to achieve his final confirmed victories. Late the following morning MK777 was flown by Flg Off Larry Robillard on a sweep that became engaged in a large dogfight near Caen, during which he claimed one of the six Bf 109s shot down to reach ace status. Flying the aircraft later that same day, Dowding damaged an Fw 190 that proved to be his final combat claim. Like both of its pilots that day, MK777 survived the war, and it was sold to the Belgian Air Force in 1948.

# 13

**Spitfire IX NH320/9G-W of Sqn Ldr T A Brannagan, No 441 Sqn RCAF, B3 St Croix-sur-Mer, France, 13 July 1944**

On 1 July Tommy Brannagan, who had two shared victories to his name, became CO of No 441 Sqn based in Normandy. Within days he had shot down an Fw 190 and then late in the evening of the 13th, when flying NH320, he led an armed reconnaissance to the Argentan area. Spotting 12 Fw 190s, Brannagan led his men in a classic 'bounce' that resulted in ten enemy fighters being claimed destroyed. Two fell to his guns, thus taking him to acedom in some style. He continued to lead No 441 Sqn until he was downed by flak on 15 August and made a PoW. NH320 survived the war and was sold for scrapping in 1950.

# 14

**Spitfire IX MJ583/FN-D of Maj M Y Gran, No 331 (Norwegian) Sqn, Tangmere, 18 July 1944**

Operation *Goodwood* against Caen on 18 July opened with a series of large-scale heavy bomber raids, which No 331 Sqn's Spitfires helped escort. Flying this aircraft (that wore the Norwegian national colours on its spinner) that day, Maj Martin Gran led his unit aloft at 0750 hrs, but the mission proved uneventful and the aircraft landed back at 0940 hrs. MJ583 had been regularly flown by future ace 2Lt Ragnar Dogger since

February, and in it on 15 June he had shot down an Fw 190 for his fourth success. Five days later Lt Kjell L'Abee-Lund shared in the destruction of a Bf 109 near Caen whilst at the controls of MJ583. The fighter was transferred to No 83 Group Support Unit shortly thereafter. Martin Gran continued to serve post-war in the Royal Norwegian Air Force and retired as a Colonel.

## 15
### Spitfire IX NH493/FF-J of WO D J Watkins, No 132 Sqn, B14 Amblie, France, 30 July 1944
NH493, which was delivered to No 132 Sqn on 20 April 1944, was flown by Flt Sgt Desmond Watkins (who became an ace in May 1945) on an armed reconnaissance on 30 July. Although it was usually flown by Flg Off Forbes on fighter-bomber missions, the aircraft was also used operationally by another ace, Flt Lt Mike Graham, on 12 August. However, three days later, when flown by 22-year-old New Zealander Plt Off Robert Harden, it was shot down by the ever deadly enemy flak whilst strafing motorised transport near Falaise, killing the pilot.

## 16
### Spitfire IX MJ311/W2-W of Sqn Ldr R L Spurdle, No 80 Sqn, West Malling, July-August 1944
Upon moving to England in April 1944, No 80 Sqn became part of the ADGB, being equipped with Spitfire IXs. In July the unit came under the command of ten-victory ace Sqn Ldr Bob Spurdle, who subsequently flew MJ311 on a number of occasions. The fighter, which had joined No 80 Sqn in May, was decorated with the unit's bell marking (within which was the individual aircraft letter) on its nose. Spurdle's first flight in the fighter came on 31 July when he led a 12-aircraft escort for Lancasters bombing a tunnel at Chigny from 18,000 ft. His last flight in MJ311 came on 13 August when he helped cover an attack on Trouville by USAAF A-20s and B-26s. No 80 Sqn received Tempest Vs later that same month, whereupon MJ311 was transferred to No 310 Sqn. It was written off in a training accident whilst serving with the unit on 3 September, killing the pilot.

## 17
### Spitfire IX ML296/DU-N of Flt Lt O Smik, No 310 (Czechoslovak) Sqn, Digby, July-September 1944
With ten aircraft and three V1s destroyed, Otto Smik was the most successful Czechoslovak pilot to fly the Spitfire. In July 1944 he became a flight commander in No 312 Sqn, and Smik was allocated ML296. In addition to the unit badge on the nose, the fighter was also marked with the Czech roundel under the cockpit and Smik's impressive personal scoreboard. On 3 September he was flying ML296 when he provided fighter escort for a daylight Halifax raid to Soesterberg, in Holland. He then conducted a strafing attack on Gilze-Rijen airfield. There, Smik reportedly destroyed two Ju 88s on the ground before being hit by flak. He successfully crash-landed and evaded capture, returning to action the following month. However, on resuming operations as the CO of No 127 Sqn Smik was killed when he was shot down by flak attacking a railway goods yard near Arnhem on 28 November.

## 18
### Spitfire IX MH910/RF-G of Flt Lt E Szaposznikow, No 303 (Polish) Sqn, Westhampnett, August 1944
In early 1944 Battle of Britain ace Eugeniusz Szaposznikow joined No 303 Sqn, and in July he became a flight commander. Part of the ADGB, as the summer progressed No 303 Sqn

began escorting daylight raids by Bomber Command, Throughout August Szaposznikow regularly flew MH910, which was decorated with the unit badge beneath the cockpit and the customary Polish chequers on its nose. In October he left for a staff post, and MH910 did not last long following his departure for during an armed reconnaissance over Holland on 1 November the fighter was hit by flak while strafing barges and crashed at Hemburg, northwest of Amsterdam. Its pilot, Sgt Jan Wierchowicz, was killed.

## 19
### Spitfire IX MK734/DL-C of Flt Lt J W P Draper, No 91 Sqn, Deanland, August 1944
Having exchanged its Griffon-engined Spitfire XIVs for Merlin-engined Mk IXs, No 91 Sqn resumed operations on the evening of 11 August when it escorted Lancasters to the Douai area. Canadian John Draper, who was an ace against both aircraft and V1s, flew MK734 during this mission. The next day it was flown by fellow V1 ace Flt Lt Ken Collier, and on 28 August by the Wing Leader, Wg Cdr Bobby Oxspring. Over the next few months MK734 was a regular participant in long-range escort missions, being flown by a number of No 91 Sqn's notable pilots and seeing considerable action. On 21 and 26 September, V1 aces Flt Lt A R Elcock and Sqn Ldr P M Bond (then No 91 Sqn's CO) flew it when escorting re-supply transports into the maelstrom at Arnhem. Then near De Weel, in Holland, during another escort on 5 December, Flg Off Faulkner shot down a Bf 109. This veteran aircraft was transferred to the French Air Force after the war.

## 20
### Spitfire IX MK520/3W-K of Flg Off J Jonker, No 322 (Dutch) Sqn, Deanland, August 1944
Having re-equipped with Spitfire IXs a few days earlier, on 12 August the Dutch-manned No 322 Sqn carried out its first 'Rodeo' when it escorted Lancasters to Orléans. Flying this aircraft was one of its V1 aces, Flg Off Jan Jonker, who fell out of formation with engine trouble and managed to force land safely at Rennes. However, his good friend, and the squadron's leading V1 ace, Flg Off Rudi Burgwal (in 3W-L) who broke off to cover him was never heard of again. Jonker soon returned to action. MK520 had only been on the squadron long enough to have the unit codes applied (but not the usual Dutch orange triangles) when it participated in the 12 August mission. The fuselage serial number that had been overpainted was reapplied on the fin in small white characters. This aircraft was transferred to No 326 (French) Sqn in September 1944.

## 21
### Spitfire IX MK984/ZF-R of Sqn Ldr W Rettinger, No 308 (Polish) Sqn, B10 Plumetôt and B31 Londonières, France, August-September 1944
After escaping to England in 1941 Witold Rettinger joined No 308 Sqn, with whom he made all his victory claims that same year. On 21 March 1944 he returned to No 308 Sqn as its CO, and during the summer he flew MK984 regularly on operations over Normandy. As well as carrying the name *Lala* ('Doll'), the aircraft also bore an impressive bomb log on the port side of the nose – No 308 Sqn was mostly engaged in fighter-bomber work following the D-Day invasion. In November Rettinger left for a staff post, whilst MK984 was destroyed on the ground at B61 St Denis-Westrem during the Luftwaffe's attack on New Year's Day 1945. It was still assigned to No 308 Sqn at the time.

## 22
### Spitfire IX MK805/SH-B of Sqn Ldr C P Rudland, No 64 Sqn, Bradwell Bay, 5-8 September 1944

MK805 was one of the first Spitfire IXs delivered to No 64 Sqn when the unit re-equipped with the aircraft for the second time in June 1944 (it had initially flown them from June 1942 through to March 1943, before switching back to Spitfire VBs). It soon became the regular mount of Flg Off Tony Cooper, who named it *Peter John III* after his two-month-old son. He first flew it on a 'Jim Crow' patrol on 7 July and on defensive and offensive operations thereafter. As seen here, No 10 Group ADGB squadrons adorned their fighters with very narrow AEAF stripes. As these usually covered the individual aircraft letter, this was repeated on the rudder, as was the case with MK805. In August Sqn Ldr Cliff Rudland (a successful Whirlwind pilot with two aerial and seven ground victories to his name) was appointed as CO, and in early September he flew MK805 several times on operations over Holland. The first was on the evening of the 5th, when Rudland led a sweep to Utrecht, and the last was three days later when he flew on Operation *Big Ben*, looking for V2 rockets. Supplied to the Italian Air Force in 1946, MK805 survives to this day as an exhibit in the *Aeronautica Militaire* Museum at Vigna di Valle, on Lake Bracciano (near Lazio), in central Italy.

## 23
### Spitfire MJ448/YO-W of Sqn Ldr R I A Smith, No 401 Sqn RCAF, B68 Le Culot, Belgium, 29 September 1944

Rod Smith, who had become an ace over Malta in 1942, resumed operations in April 1944 and flew throughout the action-packed summer of that year. In late September he was promoted to command No 401 Sqn at Le Culot, which post-war became better known as Beauvechain Air Base. On his first patrol with his new unit early on 29 September, Smith and his squadronmates became embroiled in heavy fighting over Nijmegen – No 421 Sqn was also involved. During the action No 401 Sqn pilots claimed nine aircraft shot down and five damaged, with two Bf 109s falling to Smith to take his total to 13. Two Messerschmitts also fell to Flt Lt Hedley Everard, who was thus elevated to acedom. Smith returned to Canada in November, whilst MJ448 survived the war and was eventually sold to Turkey in 1947.

## 24
### Spitfire IX ML214/5J-K of Sqn Ldr J A Plagis, No 126 Sqn, Bradwell Bay, July-December 1944

Johnny Plagis was the highest scoring Rhodesian fighter pilot of World War 2, and in July he was made the CO of No 126 Sqn. Shortly afterwards he adopted ML214 as his own Spitfire, and flying it on 24 July he shot down a Bf 109 near Angers. Then, during an eventful sortie on 14 August, Plagis destroyed another Bf 109 (and damaged a second) and downed an Fw 190 whilst at its controls. His last operational sortie in this aircraft was on the afternoon of 7 October when he flew a 'Ramrod' escorting bombers to Emmerich. Although it received Category B damage during the mission, ML214 was repaired and returned to the unit in mid-November. Thereafter, Plagis flew other aircraft on operations but may have occasionally flown this fighter on non-operational sorties until he left at the end of the year. ML214, decorated with Plagis' impressive scoreboard, was named after his sister Kay. Under the Imperial gift scheme, No 126 Sqn was the 'Persian Gulf' gift unit, with some of its aircraft being named after local Sultanates – ML214 was christened *Muscat*. Shown as it

appeared in mid December 1944, this fighter was also supplied to the French Air Force post-war.

## 25
### Spitfire IX ML365/JW of Gp Capt P R Walker, No 135 Wing, B65 Maldeghem, Belgium, November 1944

'Johnnie' Walker was a pre-war RAF pilot who became an ace during the Battle of France, and by late 1944 he commanded No 135 Wing in 2nd TAF, with fellow ace Wg Cdr Ray Harries as the wing leader. Walker occasionally flew on operations with his squadrons, and had his own personally marked Spitfire IX that not only bore his initials but also wore a nose marking that appears to be a depiction of the famous *Johnnie Walker* whisky label. Walker remained in command of the Wing until the end of the war, whilst ML365, which was on the 'books' of Nos 349 and 485 Sqns, also survived and is believed to have been transferred to France post-war.

## 26
### Spitfire FR IX MJ966/J of Flt Lt W Sawers, No 414 Sqn RCAF, B78 Eindhoven, Holland, 24 December 1944

In response to No 39 Wing's requirement for a combat-worthy camera-equipped aircraft to replace its Mustang Is, No 511 Field Repair Unit developed the Spitfire FR IXC reconnaissance conversion. This involved modifying the radio compartment through the fitment of a camera window fairing on either side of the fuselage of existing donor Spitfire IXC airframes that arrived for repair or deep maintenance. Deliveries to No 414 Sqn began in August 1944, and the FR IX proved both popular with pilots and successful in the fighter reconnaissance task. It was also more than capable of looking after itself, with reconnaissance aces Sqn Ldr Gordon Wonnacott and Flt Lt 'Sammy' Hall both achieving three victories in FR IXs. MJ966 was flown by another successful 'recce' pilot, Flt Lt Bill Sawers, who in a remarkable combat near Cologne on Christmas Eve 1944 made five claims over Bf 109s in a single sortie, three of which were confirmed and two damaged. MJ966 was also supplied to the French Air Force post-war.

## 27
### Spitfire IX MK686/DB-L of Flt Lt J J Boyle, No 411 Sqn RCAF, B88 Heesch, Holland, December 1944 to March 1945

Flying this aircraft soon after midday on 25 December 1944, 22-year-old John Boyle had the ultimate Christmas present when, over his base at Heesch as he returned from a sortie, he sighted an Me 262 jet. He had encountered one two days earlier, but had only managed to damage it. On this occasion, however, he used his superior height to build up sufficient speed to catch 9K+MM of II./KG 51 in a dive and set it on fire – the second of his six victories crashed spectacularly. The following May MK686 gained a small niche in history when, flown by Flt Lt T L O'Brien, on the 4th it shot down an He 111 to claim the last victory by a Merlin-engined Spitfire in Europe. MK686 was transferred to France in 1946.

## 28
### Spitfire IX ML119/JX-B of Sqn Ldr D G S R Cox, No 1 Sqn, Manston, January-March 1945

When David Cox assumed command of No 1 Sqn on New Year's Day 1945 he took over ML119/JX-B as his personal mount from his predecessor and fellow ace, Pat Lardner-Burke. Cox had the name *Pat* applied beneath his rank pennant. Thus adorned, the fighter was used by Cox in many of No 1 Sqn's long-range bomber escort missions and fighter sweeps through the winter of 1944-45. His last operation was covering the airborne forces drop at Wesel during the Rhine crossing in late March, after which Cox was posted to Burma. ML119 remained with No 1 Sqn until May 1945, and it was subsequently transferred to the Czech Air Force in 1946. Later sold to Israel and then Burma, the airframe still exists and is presently in storage in Kent.

## 29
### Spitfire IX PV181/RAB of Lt Col R A Berg, No 132 Wing, B79 Woensdrecht, Holland, January 1945

When Rolf Berg was made Wing Leader of No 132 Wing, as was the privilege of his position, he identified his Spitfire with his initials. He initially used MJ462, but in the autumn of 1944 took over this aircraft. At the same time authority had been given for French units to wear their national markings, so taking this as precedence, Berg had PV181 painted in the pre-war Norwegian striped identity markings around the wings and tail. However, approval for this change was not forthcoming and so the markings were changed to conform to standard practice. Berg was flying this aircraft when, on the afternoon of 3 February 1945, he was shot down and killed by flak when attacking an airfield in Holland.

## 30
### Spitfire XVI TD126/AU-C of Sqn Ldr J D Browne, No 421 Sqn RCAF, B90 Kleine Brogel, Belgium, March 1945

Sqn Ldr Danny Browne, an American in the RCAF, took over No 421 Sqn in late 1944 and led it until war's end. During the spring he flew this Spitfire XVI, whose markings conformed to the approved schemes but like many Canadian units it was also adorned with the squadron badge on the nose. In all Browne made six aerial combat claims, four of which were confirmed destroyed, and he was one of many for whom the sought after fifth never came. Post-war TD126 served with the Royal Hellenic Air Force.

## 31
### Spitfire XVI TB476/2I-D of Sqn Ldr A H Sager, No 443 Sqn RCAF, B90 Kleine Brogel, Belgium, March 1945

Like many of its brethren, TB476 that was delivered to No 443 on 15 March had shorter span 'clipped' wings fitted to improve low-level performance. Shortly after its arrival the fighter was flown by No 443 Sqn's CO, Sqn Ldr Art Sager, who had taken over command of the unit the previous October – just a few days after he had achieved his fourth and fifth victories on 27 September. Many of No 443 Sqn's aircraft carried names, with TB476 being christened *Ladykiller*. As was standard at the time, it wore yellow-outlined Type C1 roundels above the wings for easier identification. TB476 remained with No 443 Sqn beyond VE Day, when the spinners of the unit's aircraft were painted black and yellow as befitted the 'Hornet Squadron'. This fighter was scrapped in Germany in March 1946.

## 32
### Spitfire XVI TD324/SS of Wg Cdr R W F Sampson, No 145 (French) Wing, B85 Schindel, Holland, April-May 1945

On being appointed the leader of No 145 (French) Wing in January 1945, Sampson had the initials SS (for 'Sammy' Sampson) and his rank pennant applied to his first aircraft, RK853, in which he achieved his final victory on 13 March. The following month he took over TD324, which was a low-backed aircraft that was on the strength of No 345 Sqn. He duly flew this fighter for the remaining weeks of the war. TD324's days

ended when it crashed near Hale in October 1945. Earlier, Sampson had been one of the few pilots to carry his initials on the high-altitude Spitfire VII.

## 33
### Spitfire XVI TB756/DN-H of Flt Lt J D Lindsay, No 416 Sqn RCAF, B114 Diepholz and B154 Reinsehlen, Germany, 24-28 April 1945

James Lindsay became an ace with No 403 Sqn in the summer of 1944 and eventually joined No 416 Sqn on 20 April 1945, three days after his final claim in the Spitfire. He regularly flew TB756 after joining his new unit, the fighter being fitted with clipped wings. Lindsay's first mission in the aircraft came on 24 April when he led a patrol of the Hamburg and Bremen areas, and he was aloft again in TB756 four days later on a patrol to Hagenow. The aircraft, often fitted with a slipper tank, was also flown during this period by fellow ace Flt Lt John Harten. TB756 survived the war (it was struck off charge in 1949), as did Lindsay, who, when flying USAF F-86 Sabres over Korea, was credited with two MiG-15s destroyed and three damaged to become the Commonwealth's top-scoring pilot of the conflict.

## 34
### Spitfire XVI TB900/GE-D of Sqn Ldr R A Lallemant, No 349 (Belgian) Sqn, B106 Twente, Holland, and B113 Varrelbusch, Germany, April-May 1945

Having become an ace flying the Typhoon in 1944, Raymond Lallemant, after recovering from serious burns, was given command of his countrymen in No 349 Sqn in March 1945. Following brief service with No 127 Sqn, TB900, which had been presented in tribute to Prime Minister Winston Churchill, was delivered to No 349 Sqn at Twente. Probably because of its emotive name, the fighter was adopted by Lallemant as his own, and in addition to his rank pennant and impressive scoreboard of both aircraft and vehicles destroyed, it also wore a cockerel's head reminiscent of that carried on Fw 190s of JG 2! Unlike TB900, which was scrapped in 1946, Raymond Lallemant had a lengthy post-war flying career in the Royal Belgian Air Force, eventually retiring as a Colonel.

## 35
### Spitfire XVI TB752/KH-Z of Sqn Ldr H P M Zary, No 403 Sqn RCAF, B114 Diepholz, Germany, April-June 1945

In early 1945 'Hank' Zary assumed command of No 403 Sqn, leading it through the hectic final months of the war when the unit flew mainly armed reconnaissance sorties over the shrinking Reich. During the late afternoon of 21 April he was flying this Spitfire XVI when he shot down a Bf 109 near Schnackenburg, thus making him the final No 403 Sqn pilot to become an ace. Four days later, when flown by Flg Off David Leslie, TB752 shot down an Fw 189. Finally, on 1 May, it claimed its third kill when Flt Lt Robert Young downed a Fw 190. After the war TB752 received a coloured spinner, as depicted here. This significant aircraft has been on display in the Spitfire Memorial Museum at Manston, in Kent, since 1981.

## 36
### Spitfire XVI TD246/GRM of Gp Capt G R McGregor, No 126 Wing, B116 Wunstorf and B152 Fassburg, Germany, July-August 1945

When Gordon McGregor became an ace during the Battle of Britain he was already 39 years old! He remained in operational appointments throughout the war, serving in both

Alaska and Europe, before assuming command of No 126 Wing in July 1944. Leading the Wing for the rest of the war, McGregor continued to occasionally fly on operations – his last mission came on 28 March 1945, and he was the oldest RCAF pilot to see action. TD246 was delivered to No 126 Wing just after the end of the war when McGregor adopted it as his own, and like many other senior officers applied his initials to it. He flew the fighter until his return to Canada in September 1945, whilst TD246 ended its days with the Royal Hellenic Air Force.

# BIBLIOGRAPHY

**Bowyer, Michael**, *Fighting Colours*. PSL, 1969 and 1975

**Cossey, Bob**, *Tigers (No 74 Sqn)*. AAP, 1992

**Fergusson, Aldon**, *Beware, Beware* (No 611 Sqn). Airfield Publications, 2004

**Flintham, Vic and Thomas, Andrew**, *Combat Codes*. Airlife, 2003 and 2008

**Franks, Norman,** *The Battle of the Airfields*. William Kimber, 1982

**Franks, Norman**, *RAF Fighter Command Losses 1944-45*. Midland Publishing, 2000

**Gnys, Wladek**, *First Kill*. William Kimber, 1981

**Griffin, John and Kostenuk, Samuel**, *RCAF Squadron Histories and Aircraft*. Stevens, 1977

**Halley, James**, *Squadrons of the RAF and Commonwealth*. Air Britain, 1988

**Herrington, John**, *Australians in the War 1939-45, Series 3 Volume 3*. Halstead Press, 1962

**Houlton, Johnnie**, *Spitfire Strikes*. John Murray, 1985

**Hovey, H R and Schmidt, D**, *No 416 Sqn History*. Hangar Bookshelf, 1984

**Jefford, Wg Cdr C G**, *RAF Squadrons*. Airlife, 1988 and 2001

**Kennedy, Sqn Ldr I F**, *Black Crosses Off My Wingtip*. General Store, 1994

**MacDonald, Grant and Strocel, Terry**, *No 442 Sqn History*. Private 1987

**Matusiak, Wojtek**, *Polish Wings Vols 13, 15 and 16*. Stratus, 2011 and 2012

**McIntosh, Dave,** *High Blue Battle (No 401 Sqn)*. Spa Books, 1990

**Milberry, Larry and Halliday, Hugh**, *The RCAF at War 1939-1945*. CANAV Books, 1990

**Morgan, Eric B and Shacklady, Edward**, *Spitfire – The History*. Key Publishing, 1993

**Page, Geoffrey**, *Shot Down In Flames*. Grub St, 1999

**Rawlings, John D R**, *Fighter Squadrons of the RAF*. Macdonald, 1969

**Richards, Denis**, *RAF Official History 1939-45, Parts 2 and 3*. HMSO, 1954

**Robertson, Bruce**, *Spitfire – The story of a Famous Fighter*. Harleyford, 1960

**Sampson, Wg Cdr R W F and Franks, Norman**, *Spitfire Offensive*. Grub St, 2002

**Shores, Christopher,** *Those Other Eagles*. Grub St, 2004

**Shores, Christopher and Williams, Clive**, *Aces High Vols 1 and 2*. Grub St, 1994 and 1999

**Sturtivant, Ray et al**, *Spitfire International*. Air Britain, 2002

**Thomas, Chris and Shores, Christopher**, *2nd Tactical Air Force Vols 1 to 4*. Classic Publications, 2005-2008

**Tidy, Douglas**, *I Fear No Man (No 74 Sqn)*. Macdonald, 1972

**Walpole, Gp Capt Nigel**, *Dragon Rampant (No 234 Sqn)*. Merlin Massara, 2007

**Walsh, Tom**, *Remembering the Canadian Yanks*. PublishAmerica, 2012

**Wells, Kevin**, *The New Zealand Spitfire Squadron (No 485 Sqn)*. Hutchinson, 1984

# ACKNOWLEDGEMENTS

The author wishes to record his gratitude to the following pilots who have given of their time in presenting accounts or information for inclusion within this volume – Flt Lt Clive Anderton DFM, the late Air Vice-Marshal C W Coulthard CB AFC, the late Wg Cdr D G S R Cox DFC, the late Wg Cdr J C Freeborn DFC, Flt Lt P N G Knowles, the late Air Commodore I N MacDougal CBE DFC, the late A J Mallandaine, the late Wg Cdr O L Hardy DFC and bar and Flt Lt W B Peglar DFC.

# INDEX